GO GRAMMAR! 3

A HOMEWORK AND IN-CLASS WORKBOOK

(Grammar) *noun*
the set of rules that explain
how words are used in a language:
speech or writing judged by how well
well it follows the rules of grammar:
a book that explains the grammar rule their
of a language: the study of the classe of words,
inflections, and thei functions and
relations in the sen b: a study of what is
to be preferred and what avoided in inflection
and syntax; the cha inflections and syntax of a languag
a system of rules th e grammatical structure of a language; a
grammar textbook speech or writing evaluated according
to its conformity to rammatical rules; the branc of
linguistics that deals syntax and morph
sometimes also phonol and semantics; th
abstract system of rules person's mastery o
his native language can be ematic description
of the grammatical facts of a language; a book containing
an account of the grammatical facts of a language or
recommendations as to rules for the proper use of a
language; the use of language with regard to its
correctness or in syntax;
the te

EDITION 4

L DERIU • P GARLICK

Go Grammar! 3
4th Edition
Laura Deriu
Pam Garlick

Publishing editor: Michael Spurr
Project editor: Mandy Herbet
Editor: Carolyn Glascodine
Proofreader: Sarah Blood
Production controller: Erin Dowling
Cover design: Leigh Ashforth, Watershed Design
Text design: Leigh Ashforth, Watershed Design
Cover image: Getty Images/Andy Bridge
Permissions researcher: Debbie Gallagher
Typset by: SPi Global

For product information and technology assistance,
in Australia call **1300 790 853**;
in New Zealand call **0800 449 725**

For permission to use material from this text or product, please email **aust.permissions@cengage.com**

ISBN 978 0 17 038952 5

Cengage Learning Australia
Level 7, 80 Dorcas Street
South Melbourne, Victoria Australia 3205

Cengage Learning New Zealand
Unit 4B Rosedale Office Park
331 Rosedale Road, Albany, North Shore 0632, NZ

For learning solutions, visit **cengage.com.au**

Printed in China by 1010 Printing International Limited.
9 10 25

CONTENTS

Parts of speech

Vocabulary

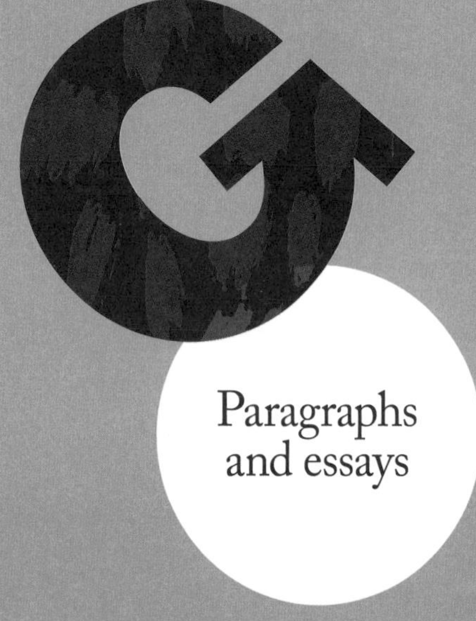
Paragraphs and essays

INTRODUCTION

The *Go Grammar!* series focuses on the language conventions of English: its grammar, spelling, punctuation, vocabulary and usage. This book uses the metalanguage of English – technical words such as 'preposition', 'clause', 'simile' or 'suffix' – that you need to know in order to discuss the way language is used in your writing, reading and viewing, and your speaking and listening.

This edition of *Go Grammar!* includes the terms and concepts that are covered in the *Australian Curriculum: English*.

Some of the concepts and exercises in this book will be familiar to you. You will be able to work through some sections quickly, revising material that you have encountered. Other sections will be new to you, and you need to be quite sure that you understand each new concept before moving on to the next unit. Ask your teacher to provide exercises for extra practice if you think you need them.

Mastering these units of work will make you a better writer, reader, viewer, speaker and listener. It will also assist you in facing tests such as NAPLAN with more confidence.

Each unit is organised into three sections:

EXPLANATION
You will find this box at the beginning of each unit. Sometimes there is a second explanation box later in the unit, to teach you another part of the topic. Memorise these sections.

HAVE A GO exercises: These exercises allow you to practise what you have read and memorised in the explanation. For example, you might need to show that you can identify a part of speech or that you can correctly punctuate a sentence.

TAKE IT FURTHER exercises: These exercises are usually more challenging, allowing you to check that you really understand the topic.

You will also find in this book:

REVISION TESTS: Use these tests to make sure that you have understood the work you have done in the preceding units.

SPELLING FOCUS sections: Many units in *Go Grammar 3!* include spelling focus activities. Use these exercises to consolidate your knowledge of the spelling of English.

Answers to all the exercises in this book are available for your teacher. When there is more than one possible response, we suggest that you work with a partner to check each other's answers. Working with a partner is a good way of making sure that you have understood every topic.

We hope you enjoy working through the exercises in this book and discover new and interesting things about grammar.

AUTHOR ACKNOWLEDGEMENTS

Much gratitude to my teaching colleagues and students, and the editorial team; as well as Karen, Harry, Nina and Tara

Laura Deriu

This is dedicated to the many students from whom I have learnt so much over the years, and to Bez, David and James who are so supportive of all my work.

Pam Garlick

Name: | Due date: | Guardian signature:

1 NOUNS

Parts of speech

A **noun** is a naming word for a person, place, creature, thing, quality, idea or feeling. There are four types of nouns.

→ A **common noun** is a naming word for a person, place, creature or thing.

e.g. dog, football, tree, boy, mother

→ A **proper noun** is a naming word for a particular person, place, thing, business or organisation. A proper noun always begins with a capital letter.

e.g. *Names/nicknames:* Anna Fiori, Ms Hayes, Buddy
Titles of people and books: Professor Susie Foster, Captain Starlight, *To Kill a Mockingbird*
Place names: Perth, Lake Eildon, Alice Springs
Subjects: English, History, Maths
Special days: New Year's Day, Remembrance Day

→ An **abstract noun** is a naming word for a quality, an idea or a feeling.

e.g. love, health, kindness

→ A **collective noun** is a naming word for a group or collection of people, animals or objects.

e.g. team, audience, litter

Collective nouns are usually considered singular and require the use of a singular verb.

e.g. The *flock* of sheep *was* moved from the top paddock.
The *audience* conveyed *its* displeasure by booing the performer.

Any of these four types of nouns can be compound nouns. A **compound noun** is made up of two or more elements.

e.g. court martial, brother-in-law, passer-by

The plural forms of these nouns are unusual because we are referring to more than one *court*, more than one *brother* and more than one *passer-by*.

e.g. courts martial, brothers-in-law, passers-by

For plurals of other compound nouns, simply add an –s.

e.g. mouthful → mouthfuls; grown-up → grown-ups

1 Complete the table on the next page by identifying the types of nouns in the text below. Do not include nouns used as adjectives, such as *ambulance*.

> Grabbing his medical bag, Doctor Phillips leapt out of his car at the scene of the accident. He fought his way through the crowd gathered around the crumpled pile of metal that only minutes ago had been a blue car. He moved toward the driver's door, already searching for signs of life behind the square red-and-white plate. He knew that the ambulance crew would be here soon, but he also knew with certainty that he would have much to do before its arrival.

Nouns are mostly used in noun groups, which are clusters of words built around the main noun or head word.

Common	Proper	Abstract	Collective

2 Write the abstract nouns for the word families in the following table.

Abstract noun	Verb	Adjective	Adverb
	admire	admirable	admirably
	amaze	amazing	amazingly
	anger	angry	angrily
	beautify	beautiful	beautifully
	embitter	bitter	bitterly
	amuse	amusing	amusingly
	brave	brave	bravely
	caution	cautious	cautiously
	embolden	bold	boldly
	empathise	empathetic	empathetically
	equalise	equal	equally
	free	free	freely
	grieve	grievous	grievously
	hate	hateful	hatefully

The easy way to tell whether a word is a noun is to try to fit it into one of these sample sentences. If it fits, it is a noun.

(The) ______________ is good. (The) ______________ are good.

3 Which of the words below can be used as a noun? Underline them.

canary	gallops	kookaburra	sings
clown	gently	laughter	soars
discreetly	giraffe	outrageously	sweetly
elegant	grand	quite	titters
elephant	horrible	raining	tree
exorbitantly	humorous	rumbles	uproariously
extravagantly	inquisitive	schoolboy	yellow

4 Some common suffixes or word endings are used to make nouns. Write three examples of nouns that use the suffixes below.

Suffix	Examples
–ance	
–er	
–ess	
–ism	
–tion	
–ment	

Nominalisation is often found in formal writing, especially academic writing. Nominalisation involves the changing of other parts of speech, especially verbs, into nouns. This leads to denser and more concise sentences. It also takes the focus of attention away from the action and the person(s) responsible for the action and places it on the concept or process itself.

The councillors discussed future urban consolidation. A journalist reported on their discussion in the paper the next day.

becomes

A council discussion of future urban consolidation was reported in the paper the next day.

In each of the following pairs of sentences, underline the one that is an example of nominalisation.

a i The weather bureau has forecast high temperatures next week. Volunteer firefighters are on alert.

ii Weather bureau forecasts of high temperatures next week have put volunteer firefighters on alert.

b i Scientists have observed annual changes in temperature and analysed the results.

ii Observations of annual temperature changes have been the subject of analysis.

c i A judgement of your test performance will determine your selection.

ii You will be judged by how you perform in the test. That will determine whether you will be selected.

d i New procedures were established to increase production.

ii The establishment of new procedures resulted in an increase in production.

e i Whole villages were destroyed in the civil war. Many thousands of people were forced to flee.

ii The destruction of whole villages in the civil war forced the flight of many thousands of people.

f i The Indonesian invasion of East Timor in 1975 resulted in 25 years of occupation.

ii Indonesia invaded East Timor in 1975 and occupied the country for 25 years.

1 Singular nouns are made plural in a variety of ways, depending on how the singular noun is spelt. Apostrophes are not used when making a noun plural.

a Write the plurals under the nouns in the table below. The first two have been done for you.

b Add one more word of your own to each column, then write the plurals.

Nouns ending in *–o*: add *–s* or *–es*	Nouns ending in vowel *+y*: add *–s*	Nouns ending in consonant *+y*: becomes *ies*	Irregular nouns	Foreign nouns
dingo	donkey	lady	man	criterion
dingoes	donkeys			
hero	valley	cherry	woman	medium
mango	storey	reply	mouse	vertebra
piano	monkey	story	foot	fungus
cello	chimney	fly	half	peninsula
logo	convoy	enemy	sheep	nucleus

2 For nouns that have been taken from other languages, the plural is formed either as in the original language or (increasingly) by adding *-s* or *-es*, as in English. Complete this table:

Singular	Plural (foreign)	Plural used in English
appendix		
bacterium		
crisis		
criterion		
formula		
syllabus		
platypus		
genius		

2 PRONOUNS

Parts of speech

A **pronoun** is a word used in place of a noun.

 *He* can play football.

You were with *us* that day.

This unit deals with four types of pronouns: personal, possessive, interrogative and reflexive.

→ A **personal pronoun** is used in place of a noun that names people, animals or things. Personal pronouns can be used as the subject or object; that is, a pronoun can be the subject (doer) or the object (recipient) of the verb's action.

	Subject		Object	
Person	Singular	Plural	Singular	Plural
1st	I	we	me	us
2nd	you	you	you	you
3rd	he, she, it	they	him, her, it	them

e.g. (used as the subject) *She* gave the cake to Peter.

(used as the object) Kate gave the cake to *him*.

→ **Possessive adjectives** and **possessive pronouns** are used to show ownership.

Possessive adjective	Possessive pronoun
my	mine
your	yours
his, hers, its	his, hers, its
our	ours
your	yours
their	theirs

e.g. These are *her* music books.

The music books are *hers*.

→ **Interrogative pronouns** ask a question.

e.g. *Who* will take this path?

Whose is that?

To *whom* are you speaking?

Pronouns are one of the most important links in a text, providing unity and coherence.

→ **Reflexive pronouns** are formed by adding *–self* or *–selves*.

Singular	Plural
myself	ourselves
yourself	yourselves
himself, herself, itself	themselves

e.g. Peter went to the film by *himself.*
She hurt *herself* badly.

Pronouns are very important in ensuring that writing and speech are cohesive. They are one of the most common cohesive links.

1 Underline all the pronouns.

- **a** He tore his shirt.
- **b** Her case had been unopened since her arrival.
- **c** It was a prize for me.
- **d** My sister writes short stories.
- **e** A stray dog followed him.
- **f** He wanted to be by himself.
- **g** She brought their tickets with her.
- **h** Her father eventually fixed it for her.
- **i** He clutched his baseball bat tightly.
- **j** The team won its match.

2 Write the correct possessive pronouns or adjectives in these sentences. Use the directions in brackets as a guide.

- **a** That is ________________ magazine. (first person singular)
- **b** The surfer lost ________________ board on the first wave. (third person masculine)
- **c** It's always been a goal of ________________ to win this series. (third person feminine)
- **d** Go to the website to register ________________ opinion. (second person)
- **e** That camera is ________________. (third person feminine)
- **f** That camera is ________________. (first person singular)

3 For each of the examples in exercise 2, state whether you wrote a *possessive pronoun* or a *possessive adjective*.

- **a** ________________________________
- **b** ________________________________
- **c** ________________________________
- **d** ________________________________
- **e** ________________________________
- **f** ________________________________

A **relative pronoun** relates to the noun or pronoun that precedes it.

 The cricketers *who* are playing are the candidates for Australia.

It can also be used to link two or more simple sentences to make a single complex one.

 The bowler bowled bouncers in the poor light. The umpire suspended play.

becomes

The umpire was forced to suspend play due to the bowler *who* bowled bouncers in the poor light.

Different types of pronouns are used to relate to different things.

Pronoun	What the pronoun relates to
who	people
whom	people
whose	people, animals, objects, things and abstract ideas
which	animals, objects, things and abstract ideas
that	animals, objects, things and abstract ideas

 The girl *whose* bat I borrowed is a brilliant cricketer.

The fielder, *who* ran to the boundary, slipped into the fence.

The friend with *whom* I go to the cricket is a One-Day fanatic.

I sat on the chair, *which* was already broken.

Where is the magazine *that* I brought with me?

The cattle, *whose* feed had been destroyed, were starving.

Antecedents are the words to which the pronouns refer.

e.g. *The girl* whose bat I borrowed is a brilliant cricketer.

The fielder, who ran to the boundary, slipped into the fence.

1 Underline the relative pronouns and circle the antecedents in these sentences.

a The horses, which had been working since dawn, were very hungry.
b The test match, which had been delayed by bad weather, ended in a draw.
c The cupcakes that are on the table must not be eaten yet.
d The ground conditions, which were not ideal, did not deter the captain of the team.
e The jockeys for whom he speaks are unhappy with the track surface.
f The dancers, who had acknowledged the applause, had already returned to the dressing rooms.
g The friend for whom they were organising the party knew nothing about it.
h Her younger brother, to whom she gave the paints, completed the portrait.
i The student at whom the cheering was directed grinned in delight.

2 Write the correct relative pronouns in these sentences.

a This is the horse ________________ won the Melbourne Cup.
b My brother, with ________________ I go to the football, always barracks for Carlton.
c The cat, ________________ coat had been brushed, was sleeping soundly.
d My jacket, ________________ I lost at hockey practice, was brand new.
e She said the boy ________________ had painted that mural was only 11 years old.

3 Underline the interrogative pronouns and circle the reflexive pronouns in these sentences.

- **a** Whom did you email about the problem?
- **b** Who replied to your email?
- **c** The cat outside the window was preening itself.
- **d** You say that you have lost your book. Whose is this, then?
- **e** You will leave yourself open to suspicion if you behave like that.
- **f** I need to write myself a note.
- **g** I bought myself two new coats. Which do you prefer?

A common error in writing is to use pronouns whose antecedents are not clear.

e.g. Jane told Emma that she was very insecure.

In the example above, *who* is insecure, Jane or Emma? The sentence must be rewritten.

e.g. Jane confessed to Emma that she was feeling insecure. *or* Jane accused Emma of being insecure.

4 Rewrite each of the sentences below so that the meaning is clear.

- **a** My folder was in Mum's car, but now it's gone.
- **b** The Italian players just defeated the Spanish players and they had huge crowd support.
- **c** Thomas told his father that his shirt had a button missing.

SPELLING FOCUS

Incorrect use of apostrophes with possessive adjectives or possessive pronouns is a common spelling mistake. This is understandable because we associate the apostrophe with possession. However, the apostrophe is only correct in relation to nouns. Look back at the table of possessive adjectives and pronouns. None of them has an apostrophe – ever!

What confuses some writers even more is that some of these words are similar to other words that *do* have an apostrophe: *it's* = *it is* or *it has*; *there's* = *there is* or *there has*.

Underline the words that need an apostrophe.

- **a** Its obvious that the cat has hurt its paw.
- **b** Theres no doubt that these shoes are theirs.
- **c** The team will celebrate its win even though its now midnight.
- **d** Ah, theres the problem.

Name: | Due date: | Guardian signature:

3 VERBS

Parts of speech

A **verb** is usually an action or a doing word. Most verbs describe physical or mental actions.

Some verbs are made up of an auxiliary (helper) and a present or past participle following the auxiliary.

Linh *is helping* the charity workers distribute food. (*Is* is the auxiliary; *helping* is the present participle.)

Are you *coming* to my party? (*Are* is the auxiliary; *coming* is the present participle.)

Jason *has eaten*. (*Has* is the auxiliary; *eaten* is the past participle.)

They *had gone* to the cricket match. (*had* is the auxiliary; *gone* is the past participle.)

To check whether a word can be used as a verb try using it in this sentence:

They can ______________________.

The two most common sentence patterns in English are:

- subject–verb (S–V)
- subject–verb–object (S–V–O).

A verb that has an object is called a **transitive verb**. A verb without an object is called an **intransitive verb**.

Transitive	Intransitive
She *shook* the book.	She *shook* like a leaf.
The children *spread* the news.	The searchers *spread* out.
Have you *eaten* the chocolates?	*Have* you *eaten*?

Some verbs are always transitive and some verbs are always intransitive; other verbs can be either, depending on their use.

1 Underline the verbs in these sentences.

- **a** The cat caught the mouse.
- **b** The glider flew effortlessly through the clouds.
- **c** Was he asked the right questions?
- **d** The coach suggested that the team jog around the oval.
- **e** The doctor's bag was placed in the ambulance.
- **f** The lecture will be attended by many students.
- **g** Keep that rope taut!
- **h** The office worker was walking to the train station.
- **i** Have you eaten at that restaurant before?
- **j** The two boys ran home.

Strong, well-chosen verbs are important in the writing of narratives.

To check whether a verb is transitive or intransitive, ask *whom?* or *what?* after the verb.

e.g. The cat caught the mouse.

(The verb is *caught*. The cat caught whom or what? *The mouse*. So *caught* is a transitive verb.)

The office worker was walking to the train station.

(The verb is *was walking*. The office worker was walking whom or what? You cannot answer that question, because there is no object. So *was walking* is intransitive.)

2 Underline the transitive verbs; that is, the ones that have an object. (Some of these sentences do not contain any transitive verbs.)

- **a** The bill includes GST.
- **b** The train arrived in the city very late.
- **c** Security services in the two countries have interlinked their databases.
- **d** Major roads, train lines and an airport will interlink to ensure efficient transport.
- **e** The sound of his voice carried through the railway carriage.
- **f** He carried a very heavy suitcase.
- **g** He left in a hurry.
- **h** The courier left a parcel for you.
- **i** The class watched while the teacher demonstrated the experiment.
- **j** The class watched the video.
- **k** A lone hyena was sniffing around.
- **l** A lone hyena was sniffing the rubbish bags behind the tents.

Verbs can be *active* or *passive*. A verb is active when its subject is the 'doer' of the action.

The gale force winds *lashed* the coastline.

The rippling waves *lapped* the shore.

When a verb is passive, the subject 'receives' the action. In the following examples the coastline and the shore are the 'receivers' of the action.

The coastline *was lashed* by the gale-force winds.

The shore *was lapped* by the rippling waves.

Passive verbs are not always the best way of expressing an idea but use of the passive voice can be appropriate in formal writing, and passive verbs are frequently used in legal documents, scientific writing and official notices.

Trespassers *will be* prosecuted.

The passive voice is also useful to convey a sense of powerlessness or a character's status as a victim.

He *was* brutally *attacked*.

Many companies now ensure that documents for customers are in plain English so that these documents are easy to understand. One of the techniques that writers of such documents use is changing passive verbs to active verbs.

Householders are advised that their policy will be void if their property is inadequately secured.

becomes

You must make sure that you keep your property locked.

1 Change the passive verbs in the following sentences to active, making your sentences as clear as possible.

a Changes are being implemented in the school timetable.

b Experiments will be conducted by scientists around the world to test the latest findings.

c The film has been totally re-edited by the director for this new director's cut.

d Serious action to remedy the problem is being considered by the council.

e Traces of gold have been detected in the river by prospectors.

2 Rewrite the following passage in the active voice.

PLANTING A TREE

Before actual planting occurs, the ground must be carefully prepared. To do this, it is necessary that a hole be dug, roughly twice the diameter of the root ball and deep enough to come up to the base of the trunk. Fertiliser should be sprinkled around the plant in order to give the roots a good, healthy start.

One of the most common errors in writing is the inappropriate change of tense. This often happens in narrative writing. We might begin the story in the past tense but then become so involved with the action that we slip into the present tense without realising.

3 Rewrite the following passage, replacing any verbs that are in the wrong tense.

I was waiting in line at the bank. Suddenly, a masked figure burst through the door. 'Everyone – down on the floor now!' he says. I threw myself on the floor. A woman near the door tries to run and he threatens to shoot her. She put her hands up and lay down on the floor. The masked man jumps over the counter and holds the gun at the teller's head. Just then a police siren blasts and a car screeches to a halt outside the bank. The robber drops the gun and rushed for the back door.

SPELLING FOCUS

Below is a table of some irregular verbs. Write the past tense form and the past participle of each verb. Make sure you check the spelling. The first one has been done for you.

Present	Past	Past participle
blow	blew	blown
come		
forget		
write		
wear		
bite		
creep		
lose		
draw		
kneel		
slink		
swell		
breed		
teach		

Name: Due date: Guardian signature:

4 ADJECTIVES AND ADVERBS

Parts of speech

ADJECTIVES

An **adjective** is a word that describes a noun or a pronoun and adds to its meaning. It qualifies the noun or pronoun by describing it in terms of its shape, size, texture or colour.

The rugby field was *square*. (shape)
The *large* dogs snarled. (size)
He painted on *rough* canvas. (texture)
It was a *red* book. (colour)

We can use adjectives to compare one object or person with another. **Comparative adjectives** are used when comparing two things, and **superlative adjectives** are used when comparing more than two things.

Tran is *smarter* than Peter. (comparing two)
Chris is the *smartest* in the group. (comparing more than two)
Samira is *more beautiful* than Fran. (comparing two)
Samira is the *most beautiful* girl in the group. (comparing more than two)

Positive	Comparative	Superlative
thin	thinner	thinnest
tall	taller	tallest
Irregular		
good	better	best
bad	worse	worst
little	less	least
many/much	more	most
far	farther/further	farthest/furthest

ADVERBS

An **adverb** tells us more about a verb, an adjective or another adverb. It modifies the verb, adjective or adverb, telling us how (adverb of manner), when (adverb of time), where (adverb of place) and to what extent (adverb of degree).

e.g.

She worked *efficiently*. (How did she work? *Efficiently*. So *efficiently* is an adverb of manner.)
He slipped *yesterday*. (When did he slip? *Yesterday*. So *yesterday* is an adverb of time.)
She searched *everywhere* for the tickets. (Where did she search? *Everywhere*. So *everywhere* is an adverb of place.)
She was *quite* sick. (To what extent was she sick? *Quite*. So *quite* is an adverb of degree.)

Note that adverbs modify not only verbs but, at times, adjectives and other adverbs.

e.g.

She was an *extremely* rash player. (*Extremely* modifies the adjective *rash*.)
He ran *very* quickly in the race. (*Very* modifies the adverb *quickly*.)

Well-chosen adjectives and adverbs give precision to writing.

Adjectival and adverbial phrases perform the same function as adjectives and adverbs. They consist of a group of words with no finite verb.

→ An **adjectival phrase** qualifies a noun.

e.g. The aroma *of fresh bread* filled the bakery. (*Of fresh bread* qualifies the noun *aroma*.)

Peter saw a huge dog *with very dark fur*. (*With very dark fur* qualifies the noun *dog*.)

→ An **adverbial phrase** modifies a verb, an adverb or an adjective.

e.g. Jan remained *behind the pillar*. (*Behind the pillar* tells us where Jan remained. It is an adverbial phrase of place, modifying *remained*.)

She behaves sensibly *most of the time*. (*Most of the time* tells us when she behaves sensibly. It is an adverbial phrase of time, modifying *sensibly*.)

1 Underline the adjectives and circle the nouns they qualify.

a The angry man shouted at the boys.

b It was a grey day.

c The oily river flowed sluggishly.

d That comedian is very funny.

2 Underline the adverbs and explain which word they modify and in what way.

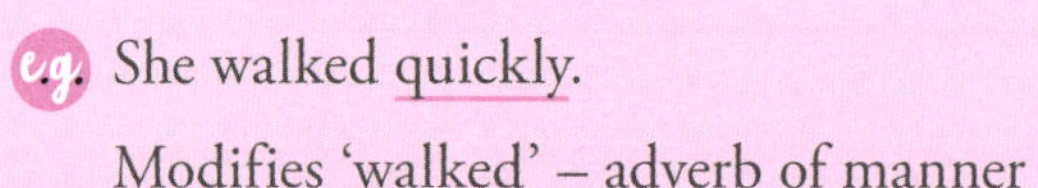

e.g. She walked quickly.

Modifies 'walked' – adverb of manner

a Julia passed her exam easily.

b They played together happily.

c They soon learnt the local customs.

d Her brother was rather tired.

e It is too hot.

f They searched everywhere for her contact lens.

g He should have gone to the market yesterday.

h He gave her the box reluctantly.

i She often comes to my house.

j He fell from his skateboard awkwardly.

3 Explain the corrections that are needed in the following sentences.

a I have one sister. I'm the smartest.

b Sydney Harbour is one of the more beautiful harbours in the world.

4 Underline the adjectives and circle the adverbs in the passages below.

EXTRACT A

Nikki bravely led the way into the dark cave. The walls were damp, with small rivulets of water running slowly down them into puddles at our feet. Our footsteps echoed loudly and the light from Nikki's torch revealed creepy shadows ahead. I had told Nikki that I wasn't scared, but I was. Very scared.

EXTRACT B

Wasif lay on his back in the spindly grass, smiling joyfully. The wind whipped the surrounding trees and blew the golden leaves this way and that. He watched the shapes pass by in the grey clouds. An old man. A pig and an emu. An ice-cream. He called out each shape to his younger sister Shiya, who was lying nearby.

1 Underline the adjectival phrases below and circle the noun or pronoun that each phrase qualifies.

a This is the lady with the large cat.
b The teacher from the other school was offended by the children's behaviour.
c The horse with no saddle galloped away.
d The tickets with the gold numbers are more expensive.
e The man in the sports car slammed on the brakes.
f I gave my ticket to the girl in the blue jacket.
g I gave my ticket to the girl wearing the blue jacket.
h The woman carrying the baby asked to see a doctor.
i The woman with the baby asked to see a doctor.
j The woman in white asked to see a doctor.

2 Underline the adverbial phrase and circle the word that the phrase modifies. After each sentence, write what kind of adverbial phrase it is.

a Not long after, Marco rushed out of the room.

b Throughout the game he shivered with cold.

c We woke before sunrise.

d He crept over to the window.

e After lunch we are going shopping.

f Meet me at the bridge entrance.

g She applauded with delight.

h He grabbed the book very abruptly.

i Kat yelled the loudest.

j Jack met his girlfriend at the cinema.

SPELLING FOCUS

Most adverbs are formed by adding the suffix *-ly* to the adjective. However, we do need to be careful about the spelling of some adverbs. Write the adverbs that are formed from the adjectives below, paying particular attention to spelling.

Adjective	Adverb	Adjective	Adverb
able		creative	
active		changeable	
admirable		comfortable	
angry		critical	
applicable		doubtful	
beautiful		merry	
brave		public	
careful		necessary	

Name: | Due date: | Guardian signature:

5 PREPOSITIONS AND CONJUNCTIONS

Parts of speech

PREPOSITIONS

A **preposition** shows the relationship between people, things and actions.

e.g. The bolt rolled *under* the motor. | The cyclist swerved *into* the oncoming traffic. | The stones scattered *across* the footpath.

Here are some common prepositions.

above	behind	down	into	out	under	within
across	below	during	like	over	up	
around	beneath	from	near	through	upon	
before	by	in	of	to	with	

There can be precise distinctions in meaning between some prepositions.

e.g. Peter agrees *with* me. | I agree *to* the deal.

There are some words that usually go with particular prepositions and it is important to learn these 'pairs'.

e.g. When you *compare* this price *with* the other one, it is clear that we should buy from this shop. (compare with) | Kevin is *dedicated to* his career. (dedicate to)

A preposition should not be confused with an adverb. A preposition shows the relationship between two things.

e.g. He sat *below* the railing.

An adverb modifies a verb, an adverb or an adjective, and it can stand alone.

e.g. He went *below*.

CONJUNCTIONS

A **conjunction** is used to join together units of language. Conjunctions can connect words, phrases or sentences.

e.g. *While* surfing the Internet, I found a website that will help me do my History homework. | *Although* his skateboard was old, it was still very fast.

Here are some common conjunctions:

after	as soon as	but	since	until	whether
although	because	for	though	when	while
and	before	or	unless	where	yet

1 Complete these sentences with appropriate prepositions.

a You can rely ______________________________ him.

b The box of tennis balls was ______________________________ the net.

Some words can be used as both prepositions and adverbs; it depends on their function in the sentence.

c Squash is different ______________________ tennis.
d George is accustomed ______________________ making his own breakfast.
e Please refrain ______________________ dropping chewing gum on the floor.
f The child is not afraid ______________________ the dogs.
g Abla was accompanied ______________________ her best friend.
h You could confide ______________________ your school counsellor.

2 In the following pairs of sentences, the same word is used twice – once as a preposition and once as an adverb. Underline the word when it is used as a preposition.

> *e.g.* I turned around to see what had caused the disturbance.
> The car turned around the corner.

a i I asked you to put that down.
ii I put the rubbish down the chute.

b i I watched him go out the gate.
ii Are you going out?

c i They were walking through some dense bush.
ii You need to push through.

d i You can have your dessert after.
ii After the main course you can have your dessert.

e i Go and stow your gear below.
ii Below deck there is plenty of storage space.

f i You'll fall behind if you don't work harder.
ii I found the book behind the couch.

g i We'll meet again by the end of the day.
ii We'll meet by the gate.

h i I'm just over the moon about our win.
ii I see that the game is now over.

3 Complete these sentences with appropriate conjunctions.

a ____________ getting soaked on the way home, the elderly man fell ill with pneumonia.
b ____________ the exams are over, we're going on schoolies' week.
c The dog hasn't been the same ____________ the rabbit joined the household.
d Sarah complained of a headache ____________ of feeling unwell.
e You don't have a chance of gaining entry to the concert ____________ you bought a ticket ages ago.
f I don't care ____________ it's sunny or snowing, I'm determined to climb that mountain!
g Do you want to visit the Davies' house ____________ stay at home?
h Patrick was frustrated ____________ he couldn't understand the work.

And, *but* and *or* are **coordinating conjunctions**; that is, they join words or clauses of equal importance.

e.g. The wind dropped *and* the sun came out.

The other team is good, *but* not good enough.

Select one *or* the other.

Conjunctions that join less important (or **subordinate**) clauses to a **principal** clause are called **subordinating conjunctions**.

e.g. I shall ask him *because* he is trustworthy.

Laura worked in the garden *until* it was nearly dark.

Each of the sentences below consists of two clauses. Underline the coordinating conjunctions and circle the subordinating conjunctions. Then, under each sentence, write each clause separately.

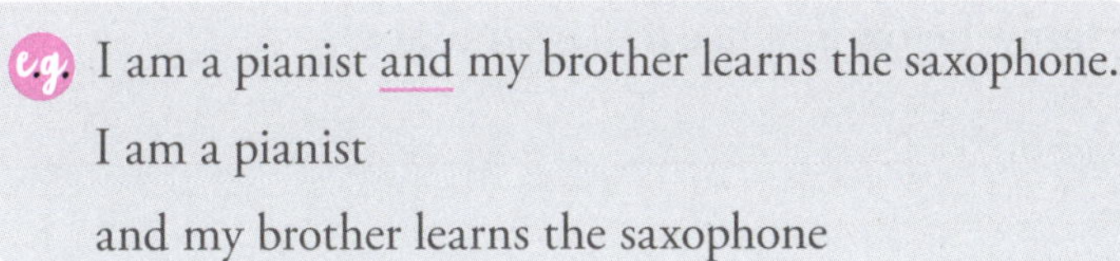

a Jane waited for the bus, but it didn't come.

b Although emus have wings, they cannot fly.

c I went to the hardware store and bought the saw, hammer and nails.

d He was reading a book when the lights went out.

e Before the doctor stitched the cut, the nurse cleaned my hand.

f Because it was time to go back to the stable, the horse trotted more quickly.

SPELLING FOCUS

1 The following words are part of the metalanguage of English; that is, the words we use when writing or talking about English as a subject. Make sure that you can spell them all. Test yourself or work with a partner and test each other.

- → adjectival
- → adverbial
- → conjunction
- → grammar
- → grammatical
- → interrogative
- → intransitive
- → metalanguage
- → participle
- → possessive
- → relative
- → transitive

2 Define each of the terms below and use it in a sentence.

a Metalanguage is: ______________________

____

b A conjunction is: ______________________

____

c A preposition is: ______________________

____

d A transitive verb is: ______________________

____

e An intransitive verb is: ______________________

____

f An active verb is: ______________________

____

g A passive verb is: ______________________

____

h An interrogative pronoun is: ______________________

____

i A participle is: ______________________

____

j A relative pronoun is: ______________________

____

Name: Due date: Guardian signature:

Parts of speech

REVISION TEST 1

1 Underline the conjunctions in these sentences.

a He rode well, but he did not win the bike race.

b They dug up the archaeological evidence before the bulldozers moved in.

c She spoke to me while she was finishing the painting.

d He will transfer to our team if he is asked.

e We want to join that gym because it is the best equipped.

f Nicholas can't transfer from his current school until the year is over.

g Although he finished the book last night, Michael did not write his report until today.

2 Replace the conjunctions in the sentences in exercise 1 with conjunctions of your own choice. Write full sentences.

a ______________________________

b ______________________________

c ______________________________

d ______________________________

e ______________________________

f ______________________________

g ______________________________

3 Circle the adjectives and underline the adverbs in these sentences.

a The small child kept white mice.

b The boys should stand in their allocated places.

c The experienced surfers waited patiently for the next wave.

d Slowly and sadly they laid the battered body of their old companion down.

e The heartless bully laughed cruelly at the obvious distress of his hapless victim.

f The drunk motorist drove erratically along the busy highway.

g The feathery smoke curled lazily from behind the distant trees.

4 Circle the pronouns and underline the possessive adjectives in these sentences.

a We will never know where she hides her money.

b Gina is a fine singer who makes her living by performing in pubs and at music festivals.

c The policeman who walks the beat is someone to admire.

d The prime minister's advisor who wrote the briefing paper was embarrassed by it.

e He used her pen to write their names in the ledger.

f The player passed the ball to his teammate and then ran forward to receive it just outside the goal line.

g He was a person whose intelligence was unquestioned.

5 Circle the verbs in these sentences and write whether they are *transitive* or *intransitive*.

a The water boiled quickly. ________________________

b John found an old wooden truck in the garden. ________________________

c The sun rises in the east. ________________________

d The loggers felled the trees. ________________________

e My friend was forced out of the group because she did not agree with the leader.
____

f He was making a kite for his sister. ________________________

g The huge man sat on the tiny chair, much to the amusement of his companions.
____

6 Complete the table using the first person singular form of the verbs as in the first row.

Present	Past	Future
break	broke	will/shall break
catch		
command		
die		
go		
ride		
run		
spell		
swim		
walk		
wander		

Name:
Due date:
Guardian signature:

6 PHRASES

Sentences

A phrase is a unit of language that does not contain a finite verb. A phrase can be used in a similar way to a noun, an adjective or an adverb.

The *overcrowded* boat was in danger of sinking.
(*Overcrowded* is an adjective, qualifying *boat.*)
The boat, *overcrowded with refugees*, was in danger of sinking.
(*Overcrowded with refugees* is an adjectival phrase, qualifying *boat.*)

The *scowling* man is my uncle.
(*Scowling* is an adjective, qualifying *man.*)
The man *with the dark scowl* is my uncle.
(*With the dark scowl* is an adjectival phrase, qualifying *man.*)

The children played *happily.*
(*Happily* is an adverb, modifying the verb *played.*)
The children played *in the garden.*
(*In the garden* is an adverbial phrase, modifying the verb *played.*)

Later we will go in for a hot drink.
(*Later* is an adverb, modifying the verb *will go.*)
After dark we will go in for a hot drink.
(*After dark* is an adverbial phrase, modifying the verb *will go.*)

Work becomes tiring.
(*Work* is a noun, the subject of the verb *becomes.*)
Working so late becomes tiring.
(*Working so late* is a noun phrase, the subject of the verb *becomes.*)

Successful *interception* is the difficulty.
(*Interception* is a noun, the subject of the verb *is.*)
Whether to intercept them is the difficulty.
(*Whether to intercept them* is a noun phrase, the subject of the verb *is.*)

I have banned *swimming.*
(*Swimming* is a noun, the object of the verb *banned.*)
I have banned *swimming in winter.*
(*Swimming in winter* is a noun phrase, the object of the verb *banned.*)

1 In each pair of sentences that follows, one sentence has an adjectival phrase. Underline the adjectival phrase.

a i I will buy some milk from the corner shop.

ii I will buy some milk from the shop on the corner.

A phrase does not contain a finite verb.

b i We will find a shady camp site.

ii We will find a camp site in the shade.

c i That whistling kettle is getting on my nerves.

ii That kettle's whistling so loudly is getting on my nerves.

d i I was frightened of the sneering bully.

ii I was frightened of the bully sneering so contemptuously.

e i The guards with their tall hats were marching past.

ii The tall-hatted guards were marching past.

f i The excited tourists took photos.

ii The tourists took photos of the marching guards.

2 In each pair of sentences below, one sentence has an adverbial phrase. Underline the adverbial phrase.

a i I will meet you there.

ii I will meet you at the game.

b i Pitch the tent quickly.

ii Pitch the tent in the shade.

c i Can you come over tonight?

ii Can you come over after dinner?

d i She barracked enthusiastically.

ii She barracked with great enthusiasm.

e i In the first place, I should like to congratulate you.

ii Firstly, I should like to congratulate you.

f i The excited tourists were watching from the balcony.

ii The excited tourists were watching the march.

3 In each pair of sentences below, one sentence has a noun phrase. Underline the noun phrase.

a i To err is human.

ii Fallibility is human.

b i Forgiveness is virtuous.

ii Forgiving completely is virtuous.

c i Riding that roller-coaster was terrifying.

ii Snowboarding was terrifying.

d i She adores eating chocolate ice-cream.

ii She adores ice-cream.

e i Lies make it worse.

ii Lying about your behaviour makes it worse.

f i Digging that hole was exhausting.

ii Digging is exhausting.

1 In the sentences below, underline any adjectival phrases and circle any adverbial phrases.

- **a** Since daybreak, he has been revving that car in frustration.
- **b** That car in the driveway has problems with its engine.
- **c** The driver of the car is a problem of greater proportions.
- **d** He drives it in a reckless manner and he seems to like disturbing others.
- **e** The lady from next door expressed her disapproval in no uncertain terms.
- **f** She stormed out of her house in her pyjamas.
- **g** She yelled at the driver with some enthusiasm.

2 Did you notice that there was one noun phrase in the sentences in exercise 1? Write the noun phrase below.

____

3 For each phrase underlined in the following sentences, write whether it is an *adjectival*, *adverbial* or *noun* phrase.

- **a** The dog in the window is a Labrador pup. ____________
- **b** Put that new stock in the window. ____________
- **c** Washing windows is hard work. ____________
- **d** Looking very smug, the captain accepted the trophy. ____________
- **e** The captain accepted the trophy before the victory parade. ____________
- **f** Winning so decisively is a triumph. ____________
- **g** The players smiled broadly because of the cheers. ____________
- **h** The captain, holding the trophy aloft, smiled broadly. ____________
- **i** The team members ran around the ground. ____________
- **j** The coach, with tears in his eyes, hugged the captain. ____________

SPELLING FOCUS

People may tell you that all you have to do to become a good speller is to learn phonetics – that is, to learn to match the sounds of the language with the letters of the alphabet. Unfortunately, because of the rich history of the English language, this does not always work. The famous playwright George Bernard Shaw used to demonstrate this by asking people to pronounce the word *ghoti*.

Have you figured it out? It's easy. Just sound it out like this: *gh* as in *cough*, *o* as in *women* and *ti* as in *devotion*. You end up with the sounds made by *f*, *i* and *sh*, so *ghoti* could sound like *fish*!

In English, some similar sounds can be represented by various different spellings.

1 Read the sentences below. Some words are missing letters. In every case, the missing letter makes the sound 'ar', as in *far*, but the spelling is different in each sentence. Write in the missing letters, then rewrite the whole word. Note: the number of spaces represents the number of missing letters.

a How f__st can you run? ________________

b Are you going to plant those bulbs in the g__ __den? ________________

c The church has an annual baz__ __r, with lots of second-hand treasures. ________________

d Cut down on saturated fats to ensure a healthy h__ __ __t. ________________

e My __ __nt is my mother's sister. ________________

f His rank in the army is s__ __geant. ________________

g The gal__ __ is a bird native to Australia. ________________

h Put h__ __f the chocolate in the refrigerator for tomorrow. ________________

i Where __ __ __ you going now? ________________

j '__ __! What lovely big eyes you have,' drooled the wolf. ________________

k Security g__ __ __ds at the door will check participants' passes. ________________

l I always eat the chocolate noug__ __ first. ________________

2 Define the following words. (Give three different definitions for *bow*.)

a i bough: ________________________________

ii bow: ________________________________

iii bow: ________________________________

iv bow: ________________________________

b i sow: ________________________________

ii sough: ________________________________

iii sew: ________________________________

c i site: ________________________________

ii sight: ________________________________

iii cite: ________________________________

Name: Due date: Guardian signature:

7 CLAUSES

Sentences

A **clause** is a group of words that contains a subject and a verb.

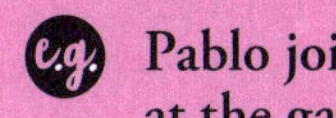

Pablo joined a golf club, // but he was no good at the game.

He cannot play golf, // although he is good at sports.

There are two types of clauses: the main (or independent) clause and the subordinate (or dependent) clause. A **main clause** usually makes complete sense on its own and expresses the main message of the sentence.

e.g. The cars sped down the track.

There can be more than one main clause, joined with conjunctions such as *and* or *but*.

e.g. The music stopped *and* the audience clapped.

main clause — main clause

When you have two (or more) main clauses like this, they are called **coordinate clauses**.
A **subordinate clause** is less important than the main clause in a sentence. It offers extra information but cannot stand alone. Subordinate clauses begin with conjunctions such as *if*, *that*, *when* and *because*, or with relative pronouns such as *who*, *whom* and *which*.

The cars sped down the track *because* the drivers were risk-takers.

main clause — subordinate clause

The subordinate clause gives extra information about the main clause.

1 In each pair of sentences below, one sentence has an underlined clause and the other sentence has an underlined phrase. (It is a phrase – not a clause – because there is no finite verb.) For each pair of sentences, write C for the sentence in which the underlined part is a clause.

a i When studying, a student should try to find a quiet room. __

ii When you are studying, you should try to find a quiet room. __

b i Since last term, I have been working hard. __

ii Since I promised my parents last term, I have been working hard. __

c i Knock before you go in. __

ii Knock before entering. __

d i The girl who is wearing the red coat is my cousin. __

ii The girl in the red coat is my cousin. __

e i I'm suspicious of the man dressed in the white dinner jacket. __

ii I'm suspicious of the man who is dressed in the white dinner jacket. __

f i After dinner you need to finish your homework. __

ii After you have had your dinner, you need to finish your homework. __

A clause must contain a finite verb.

2 Use a straight line to underline all the main clauses in the sentences below. Use a wavy line to underline all the subordinate clauses.

- **a** My cousin is studying at university, but she refuses to work hard.
- **b** She spends a lot of time partying and she is quite lazy.
- **c** When my brother was at university, he only went out on Saturday nights.
- **d** He also had to work all day on Sundays because Mum could not afford to give him an allowance.
- **e** Although he had to work hard, he did very well because he wanted to succeed.
- **f** My cousin, who is studying at university, refuses to work hard.

There are three types of subordinate clauses: noun, adjectival and adverbial. **Noun clauses** do the work of nouns.

e.g. They bought *provisions.* (noun)

They bought *what they needed.* (noun clause)

Like nouns, noun clauses can be either the subject or the object of a verb.

e.g. *What caused the bridge collapse* was never discovered.

(This is a noun clause, and the subject of the verb *was … discovered*.)

They wondered *what had caused the bridge collapse.*

(This is a noun clause, and the object of the verb *wondered*.)

Adjectival clauses qualify nouns or pronouns.

e.g. Victoria is a state *where AFL football dominates sport.*

(This is an adjectival clause, qualifying the noun *state*.)

Adverbial clauses modify a verb, an adverb or an adjective. As with adverbs, there is more than one type of adverbial clause.

e.g. They waited patiently *while the doctor treated their wounds.*

(This is an adverbial clause of time, modifying the verb *waited*.)

He pitches *as a professional would.*

(This is an adverbial clause of manner, modifying the verb *pitches*.)

Meet us *where the laneway begins to dip down the hill.*

(This is an adverbial clause of place, modifying the verb *meet*.)

We could not go waterskiing *because the river was very low.*

(This is an adverbial clause of reason, modifying the verb *could … go*.)

3 Three of the six subordinate clauses underlined in exercise 1 are adverbial clauses. Which two are adjectival clauses? Write the two adjectival clauses here.

4 Two of the sentences in exercise 2 are made up of coordinate clauses. Write those two sentences here.

5 From exercise 2, find one adverbial clause of time and one adjectival clause.

Underline and describe the clauses in the following sentences.

e.g. Emily cleaned the windows until her mother arrived home.
Adverbial clause of time, modifying the verb 'cleaned'

a He will leave after his friend has arrived.

b You will find the key where you left it.

c His friend, whom he was expecting, has now arrived.

d Her parents hoped that her hard work would be rewarded.

e We did not see the pothole because it was raining very hard.

f The helpless victim was watching the figure who was skulking around the backyard.

g Because the crocodile turned angrily, the photographers retreated.

h I thought that the film was sick.

2 The word *where* can be used to introduce all three types of subordinate clauses – noun clauses, adjectival clauses and adverbial clauses. There is an example of each one below. In the space provided, write what type of clause the *where* clause is.

a I knew where the booty was hidden.

b He found the booty in the forest where he used to go hiking.

c He hiked where the forest was dense.

SPELLING FOCUS

1 The following words are part of the metalanguage of English; that is, the words we use when writing or talking about English as a subject. Make sure that you can spell them all. Test yourself or work with a partner and test each other.

adjectival	conjunction	grammatical	punctuation	vocabulary
adverbial	coordinate	phrase	sentence	
clause	grammar	principal	subordinate	

2 Define the following words (in terms of their use in the metalanguage of English) and write each of them in a sentence.

a sentence: ______________________________

b adverbial: ______________________________

c adjectival: ______________________________

d coordinate: ______________________________

e subordinate: ______________________________

f independent: ______________________________

g punctuation: ______________________________

h vocabulary: ______________________________

Name: Due date: Guardian signature:

8 SENTENCE TYPES

Sentences

A **sentence** is a unit of language that is complete in itself. It always has a subject and a predicate.
A sentence can be a statement, a question, an exclamation or a command.

 *Statement:* Kate is walking by the riverbank.
Question: Is Kate walking by the riverbank?
Exclamation: Kate is walking by the riverbank!
Command: Kate, walk by the riverbank!

A sentence contains two basic sections: the subject and the predicate.
The **subject** is the person or thing to whom or to which the sentence refers.
The **predicate** tells us what is said or written about the subject. It must contain a verb.

Subject	Predicate
Tennis	is my favourite sport.
The boy next door	behaves badly.
Hundreds of people	perished in the earthquake.
A police officer	ran to save him.
Fish	swim.

A **simple sentence** has only one main or independent clause.

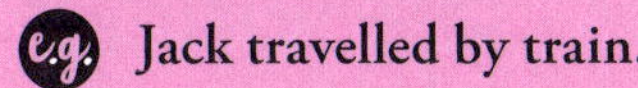
Jack travelled by train.

A **compound sentence** contains two or more main clauses.

 He travelled by train, but he did not arrive on time.
(He travelled by train — main clause; but he did not arrive on time — main clause)

A **complex sentence** contains a main clause and one or more subordinate clauses.

 Jack returned to the town where he was raised as a boy.
(Jack returned to the town — main clause; where he was raised as a boy — subordinate clause)

A **compound–complex sentence** has at least two main clauses and at least one subordinate clause.

e.g. Jack travelled by train but he did not arrive on time because the line had been blocked by a fallen tree.
(Jack travelled by train — main clause; but he did not arrive on time — main clause; because the line had been blocked by a fallen tree — subordinate clause)

A sentence begins with a capital letter and ends with a full stop, a question mark or an exclamation mark. It must contain a finite verb.

1 Underline the subject in each sentence.

- **a** Behind the couch the toddler was eating marshmallows.
- **b** James is waiting for the DVD to finish.
- **c** She poured the liquid into the beaker.
- **d** Georgie arranged the items carefully in her backpack.
- **e** This film has been shown on pay television.
- **f** After half-time the temperature increased greatly.
- **g** This is one of the more powerful laptops in the range.
- **h** The future has never looked so bright for young tennis players.
- **i** (You) Take that contraption out of here!
- **j** The first person to use anaesthetics in tooth extraction was Massachusetts dentist William Morton.

2 Identify the types of sentences as *simple*, *compound*, *complex* or *compound-complex*. If they are compound, complex or compound-complex, explain why.

- **a** The children played.
- **b** He came to dinner.
- **c** The sun shone although it was raining.
- **d** Have you met the student who worked with me on the project?
- **e** I was told that the bus would be late arriving.
- **f** The roof was removed, but the building could not be saved.
- **g** An education kit on water use is being prepared for schools.
- **h** A special meeting was convened and the local council thanked the firefighters who defended the area during the bushfires.

1 Using conjunctions or relative pronouns, combine the following sentences in the most sensible way.

a The police gave the reward to Wei. He had given them valuable assistance.

b The power went off. Marco was cooking dinner.

c Addie picked her way carefully across the room. There was broken glass everywhere.

d Marion was dedicated to her work. She was well liked by her colleagues.

e Sergio was a highly respected lawyer in Cairns. He was a very modest man.

2 Underline the predicate in each sentence.

a Millions of people on low incomes around the world are facing hunger because of rising food prices.
b A major factor in the cause of world hunger is the switch from food crops to biofuels.
c Manufacturers of genetically modified foods have claimed to have the answer to world hunger.
d Greater crop yields could come at a high price.
e More sustainable farming practices may be part of the solution.
f Sustainable farming practices can help farmers as well as consumers.
g The market for organically grown products is growing.

3 The subject of each sentence is underlined in the examples below. Each subject is an example of a noun group. Circle the main noun or head word in each subject.

a <u>Millions of people on small incomes around the world</u> are facing hunger because of rising food prices.
b <u>A major factor in the cause of world hunger</u> is the switch from food crops to biofuels.
c <u>Manufacturers of genetically modified foods</u> have claimed to have the answer to world hunger.
d <u>Greater crop yields</u> could come at a high price.
e <u>More sustainable farming practices</u> may be part of the solution.
f <u>Sustainable farming practices</u> can help farmers as well as consumers.
g <u>The market for organically grown products</u> is growing.

SPELLING FOCUS

1 You know the '*i* before *e*' except after *c* rule. Sort the list below into three groups.

- Group 1: Words that follow the '*i* before *e*' rule
- Group 2: Words that do not follow the '*i* before *e*' rule because the sound is not *ee*
- Group 3: The exceptions – words that have the *ee* sound but are spelt *ei*. (There are four exceptions in the list.)

achieve	height	priest	relief	vein
belief	leisure	protein	retrieve	weight
deceit	neighbour	receive	seize	weir
eighty	niece	rein	shriek	weird

Group 1: ______________________

Group 2: ______________________

Group 3: ______________________

Another example of English spelling that can sometimes be confusing is the use of *f* and *gh*, which can sound the same. *Ph* and *f* can also be confusing.

e.g. He was a *tough* man.
There was a *tuft* of very tall grass by the gate.
He sat down with a *humph*.

2 Write a sentence containing the word given. Then find an alternative spelling for a word that sounds the same and write it in a sentence.

a rough: ______________________

b draft: ______________________

c prophet: ______________________

Name: | Due date: | Guardian signature:

9 COMMAS, SEMICOLONS AND COLONS

Punctuation

COMMAS

Commas (,) are used to:

→ separate an introductory word, phrase or clause at the beginning of a sentence	e.g. Despite the bad weather, we went bush walking.
→ separate an explanatory word, phrase or clause within a sentence as well as separate names from titles in a sentence	e.g. The gum tree, which was more than 60 years old, collapsed in the storm. Mr Markus Vass, CEO of the company, made a speech about workplace safety.
→ separate items in a list	e.g. Please go to the supermarket and buy four potatoes, a bunch of carrots, a stick of celery and an onion.
→ separate spoken words	e.g. 'I have never been so surprised,' Mum cried.
→ separate names of people addressed	e.g. Karen, please come in. *or* Please come in, Karen.
→ separate 'Yes' and 'No' when they begin a response to a question	e.g. Do you understand the rules? Yes, but I don't agree with them.
→ separate greetings at the beginning of letters and emails (though it is increasingly common for them to be omitted)	e.g. Dear Mrs Caruso,
→ separate letter and email closings from a signature (though it is increasingly common for them to be omitted).	e.g. Yours sincerely, Dr Akin Sud

SEMICOLONS

Semicolons (;) are used to:

→ separate closely linked main clauses that are not connected by a conjunction	e.g. He could not scream; he was paralysed by fear. We forgot to download the navigation app; consequently, we were lost for most of the day.
→ separate items in a list that already contains commas.	e.g. The student delegation included Jack Singh, the Senior Prefect; Johanna Blax, the Middle School Prefect; and Sean Reilly, the Junior School Prefect. The garden contained a tall, shady, deciduous tree; several dry, round flowerbeds; a water feature; and some outdoor furniture.

COLONS

Colons (:) are used to:

→ introduce a list or a series of phrases and clauses	e.g. Please bring: a tent, a sleeping bag, a backpack and light food. The visiting chef covered the following topics: essential cooking tools, hygiene in the kitchen and food preparation tips.
→ introduce a quotation from a written or spoken text.	e.g. The editor claimed: 'The protestors will be held accountable for the massive damage caused to public property'.

Run-on sentences – when a writer uses a comma instead of a full stop to separate two separate sentences – are a common error in writing.

1 Add commas, semicolons and colons where appropriate. Use the instructions in brackets as a guide.

- **a** 75 Collinda Street Hillside NSW 2010 (2 commas)
- **b** The house which was in poor condition was demolished. (2 commas)
- **c** Morgan Cal and Lian could have gone bushwalking instead they went surfing. (2 commas, 1 semicolon)
- **d** Dear Jan I will be attending your party with my family. Kind regards Scott. (2 commas)
- **e** We were required to bring a sketchbook a pencil a ruler and an eraser. (2 commas, 1 colon)
- **f** The government has committed the country to war but there will be no public protests. (1 comma)
- **g** 'This is one of the best days of my life' said Aditi clutching her certificate. (2 commas)
- **h** The notice on the board said 'Class cancelled.' (1 colon)
- **i** Rowan please clean up after yourself! (1 comma)
- **j** There was rain and hail consequently the swimming carnival was cancelled. (1 comma, 1 semicolon)
- **k** Dr Rose Savage the chief surgeon performed the delicate operation. (2 commas)
- **l** The menu was diverse beef korma apricot chicken sausages with onion gravy vegetable lasagne and seafood pasta. (3 commas, 1 colon)

2 Add a tick next to the sentences that demonstrate correct usage of commas, semicolons and colons. Add a cross next to the sentences that show incorrect usage.

- **a** The new history textbook covers the following topics: Ancient Egypt, The Hebrews, Ancient Greece, Ancient Rome, Ancient China and Islam. _______
- **b** Anonymous is credited with saying; 'The more we share: the more we have.' _______
- **c** Yes, the rehearsal room will be available for the afternoon. _______
- **d** As the weather bureau had issued a total fire ban, the New Year's celebration fireworks were cancelled. _______
- **e** The town hall; which was more than 120 years old; was classified by the National Trust. _______
- **f** Please take a seat: Josh. _______
- **g** Dear Mr McCaskey, I am writing to request an extension for my Geography assignment. _______
- **h** I look forward to your reply: regards; Janie Moore. _______
- **i** He could not stop jogging around the oval; he was so thrilled by his unexpected victory. _______
- **j** 'I was terrified by the sudden explosion,' said an eyewitness. _______

3 One of the most common errors in writing is the use of a comma when a full stop is required. This error has occurred in two of the sentences below. Identify those sentences and then rewrite them, with correct punctuation, in the space provided on the next page.

- **a** The rehearsal room will be available, all performers need to report at two o'clock.
- **b** Performers should have memorised their roles. We will rehearse without scripts.
- **c** Understudies who are filling in for those who are away with the flu will of course be able to read their parts. All other performers are asked to provide as much support as possible for the newcomers.

d The first dress rehearsal will be held next Tuesday evening, hopefully, those who are sick will be better by then.

TAKE IT FURTHER

1 Add words, phrases and clauses to the following punctuation patterns to achieve complete sentences. Use appropriate end punctuation (. ? !).

a ______, ______

b ______, ______, ______

c ______, ______, ______ and ______

d '______,' said ______

e Kailani ______

______, ______

g ______, ______; ______, ______; ______, ______; ______, ______; and ______, ______

h ______; however, ______

i ______: '______'

j ______; consequently, ______ '______'

k ______: ______, ______ and ______

l ______; ______ ______

m ______, ______, ______: ______

2 Read this sentence:

The plants need to be pruned when necessary, regularly watered and fertilised, and cleared of bugs.

Notice that the author has placed a comma before the second use of 'and'. This is not really covered by any of the specific rules for using the comma. Why do you think the author has used a comma?

3 Consolidate your understanding of how commas, semicolons and colons are applied in real texts. Choose a fiction or nonfiction text. Select two sentences with commas, two sentences with semicolons and two sentences with colons. Copy them out and state why the punctuation has been used.

i commas:

ii semicolons:

iii colons:

SPELLING FOCUS

The following words appear in this unit. Add a tick next to the ones that are spelt correctly and a cross next to the ones that are spelt incorrectly. Write the correct spelling in the space next to the words spelt incorrectly.

seperate	[ ]		consequently	[ ]	
beginning	[ ]		develipment	[ ]	
signiture	[ ]		intamite	[ ]	
conected	[ ]		understanding	[ ]	
written	[ ]		environment	[ ]	
aproprite	[ ]		indiginious	[ ]	
comitted	[ ]		devistashing	[ ]	

Name: | Due date: | Guardian signature:

10 APOSTROPHES

Punctuation

Apostrophes (') are used to:

→ indicate a contraction – that is, the omission of a letter or letters	e.g. cannot = can't
→ indicate possession in a singular noun by adding *'s* to the noun	e.g. That is Shalini's sports bag.
→ indicate possession in a plural noun by adding the apostrophe after the *s*	e.g. the soldiers' campsite
→ indicate possession in a singular noun that already ends with an *s* by adding either *'s* or simply an apostrophe consistently	e.g. James' textbooks *or* James's textbooks
→ indicate possession in an irregular plural or collective noun by adding *'s*	e.g. the women's room, the children's playground
→ indicate possession in compound words by adding *'s* to the last word	e.g. my sister-in-law's party
→ indicate possession when two or more words show individual ownership by adding *'s* to each word	e.g. the Principal's and Deputy Principal's offices
→ indicate possession when two or more words show joint ownership by adding *'s* to the last word.	e.g. Chris and Sam's wedding.

1 Expand the contractions.

a hasn't ______
b she'd ______
c you'll ______
d they've ______
e I'm ______
f we're ______
g where's ______
h wasn't ______
i would've ______
j I'd ______
k wouldn't ______
l weren't ______
m he'll ______
n didn't ______

2 Form contractions from the following.

a it is ______
b there is ______
c should have ______
d do not ______
e let us ______
f who has ______
g are not ______
h we will ______
i could have ______
j they had ______
k you are ______
l of the clock ______

The most common punctuation mistakes are with very simple words: *it's* or *its*; *you're* or *your*; *who's* or *whose*; and *they're*, *their* or *there*.

3 Underline the words that need apostrophes and write them correctly.

a Weve been waiting for Mum and Dads visit all morning!

b The Teachers Training College is holding an Open Day.

c There will be performances of Mozarts and Chopins concertos at the Town Hall.

d The mens triathlon will be held in a weeks time.

e Its a great day for the beach. Dont forget to pack your sunscreen.

f Well be staying in my brother-in-laws caravan.

g If thats Helens laptop, wheres Jeromes laptop?

h The governments proposal wasnt accepted.

i Robin and Sues trip was cancelled due to the airlines ticketing fiasco.

j There will be a womens-only festival at Dwights camp site.

1 **a** Unfortunately, the computer has added extra apostrophes to the paragraphs below. Add ticks after the correct apostrophes and circle the unnecessary apostrophes.

Mickey looked at her boss. Des' stuffed himself into well-cut suit's to try to fit the corporate image but ended up looking like a thug, a tough's minder. He had a belly the size of a postie's sack, a double chin that wobbled like a pigeon's breast, receding sandy curl's, skin the colour of pink boiled lollies' and narrow, ice-blue eyes that were cold and blue as a shark's. When Des was furious' his anger went into his eye's and his tone stayed the same. It was an illusion, of course, one that baffled many journalists', that Des never lost his temper. He did. He just didn't show it in his' voice.

> Mickey had turned up in Des's office six month's earlier. She'd had no appointment but wheedled her way past Gwen the impregnable. Des was inclined to give her a job on the basis' of that alone. She begged him to allow her to work there; she'd do anything. She didn't even wan't to get paid. Just a toe-hold. Just a chance. Please. Des' admired Mickey's prickly determination, the persistence, the edgy resolve. She was' hungry. He'd been like that, too, once.
>
> Janine Burke 2001, *Our Lady of Apollo Bay*, Lothian, p. 1

b Write each word from the passage where apostrophes are used correctly in the correct column.

Apostrophes of contraction	Apostrophes of possession

2 Complete the table below by writing in examples of words with apostrophes from one chapter of a novel you are currently reading.

Apostrophes of contraction (add the complete form)	Apostrophes of possession (indicate whether singular or plural usage)

3 Create an apostrophe collage by cutting out examples of different types of apostrophe usage from newspaper and magazine headlines. Use colours to highlight the different uses of apostrophes. Display the collages in your classroom and refer to them when using apostrophes in your own writing. Here is an example.

4 Look out for examples of incorrect apostrophe usage – you could check advertisements, texts, social media posts. Collect five examples of incorrect apostrophe usage. Explain why each example is incorrect and correct the apostrophe use in each example.

SPELLING FOCUS

The following words appear in this unit. Add a tick next to the ones that are spelt correctly and a cross next to the ones that are spelt incorrectly. Write the correct spelling in the space next to the words spelt incorrectly.

contraction	[ ]	______	omision	[ ]	______
posesion	[ ]	______	indervidual	[ ]	______
indicate	[ ]	______	unfortunately	[ ]	______
ditermination	[ ]	______	persistance	[ ]	______
illusion	[ ]	______	apointmint	[ ]	______

Name: | Due date: | Guardian signature:

11 PUNCTUATING SPEECH

Punctuation

Quotation marks (' ') are used to:

→ enclose quoted statements such as excerpts from texts, proverbs and everyday sayings

e.g. My mother always says: 'too many cooks spoil the broth'.

→ enclose the actual words, sounds or exclamations (speech) of a speaker.

e.g. 'Wow!' Zara exclaimed. 'That's amazing!'

When punctuating speech or conversation, observe the following conventions:

→ enclose all of the spoken words in quotation marks

→ use a capital letter at the start of the first word spoken, unless it is a continuation of speech and not a new sentence

→ enclose all punctuation marks inside the quotation marks when they are part of the speaker's words

→ start a new line for each speaker.

There are several common patterns when punctuating speech – note the placement of punctuation marks, particularly the commas, in the following:

e.g. '________________________,' said the speaker.

The speaker said, '________________________.'

'________________________!' exclaimed the speaker.

The speaker exclaimed, '________________________!'

'________________________?' asked the speaker.

The speaker asked, '________________________?'

'________________________,' said the speaker. '________________________.'

1 Rewrite the following, correcting the placement of punctuation.

a 'Fine', Manoush said. 'I'll come with you'.

b 'Come on, you guys'! shouted Ali. 'What's taking so long'?

c 'I told her', Mum said, 'that she'd be in trouble if she didn't come home by 10'.

d 'May I have some cake?' I asked. 'And some cream'?

Be careful when punctuating speech, especially with the placement of commas inside or outside of the quotation marks.

2 Fill in the spaces below with appropriate speech. Note the placement of the punctuation marks.

a ‘____,’ said the football coach.

b My mother said, ‘____.’

c ‘____!’ exclaimed the shocked viewer.

d The excited student exclaimed, ‘____!’

e ‘____?’ asked his parents.

f The lady at the station asked, ‘____?’

g ‘____,’ said my music teacher. ‘____.’

h ‘____________,’ Louis said, ‘____.’

3 Add quotation marks where required in the text below.

Spring. The wrong time of year again.

Don’t forget to wrap the flowers, Beth, Mum called, and I could tell from the tight sound in her voice how she was feeling. It was how I felt, too, waiting by the front door, the flowers cradled in both arms.

I’ve wrapped them, I called back.

Outside the Sydney morning was full of light and wind. Sort of carefree. Different entirely from the atmosphere inside the house. Different from Dad who was stomping up and down the passage, jangling his keys.

Come on, you lot! he shouted. At this rate we’ll never get there.

Coming, Mum answered.

And then: Who says we have to go?

It was Sam, standing at the top of the stairs, not even half-ready to leave, his face oddly blank. He’d been told to put on his school clothes, but he was barefoot, his hair uncombed, and he was wearing a T-shirt and the oldest pair of shorts he could find.

What? Dad said, more surprised than angry, because Sam wasn’t the type of kid who made trouble.

Why can’t we go to the beach instead?

Mum hurried from the living room. Sam, she murmured warningly.

But it was as if he hadn’t heard her. There’s no one out there, he said dully. Just some old dirt and grass. Why bother going? He answered his own question by walking back along the passage to his room.

That’s when I realised something was seriously wrong.

Did you hear him? Dad shouted. Did you hear what he said?

He’s upset, Des, that’s all.

Upset! How does he think the rest of us feel?

But he’s a child.

Sam. A child. Try telling that to his computer.

Mum frowned and stepped up to him. This isn't the way to handle things, Des, she said calmly. Today especially.

Dad's face had gone all red, so I guessed what was coming next. What Mum calls one of his little boy tantrums.

Kelleher, Victor 1992, *Del-Del*, Red Fox, Random House, p. 3.

1 There are many different words that can be used to describe the way someone says something. Use a thesaurus and add words to each column.

Statement	Exclamation	Question
remarked	shrieked	interrogated
explained	screamed	requested
complained	roared	asked

2 Use the punctuation patterns that were explained above to write your own sentences. Remember to incorporate direct speech.

3 Make a list of the characteristics of real speech. Give examples to illustrate the characteristics you have identified.

4 Geoff and Lydia are teachers at a high school. The school is about to break up for the holidays. Read the section of dialogue set out as a play script then rewrite their dialogue in prose form (as in novels) on the next page, punctuating the speech correctly. You might like to include descriptions about how Geoff and Lydia speak and how they act. Try out different speech punctuation patterns for variety.

GEOFF: We only have to last until three o'clock tomorrow.

LYDIA: I can't wait. It's been such an exhausting term.

GEOFF: No more marking for six weeks!

LYDIA: Didn't you say that you were spending a couple of weeks of the holidays on a course?

GEOFF: Yes, but that will be fun.

LYDIA: Fun! It sounds like hard work to me. I'm going to spend a lot of time just lying on the beach.

GEOFF: Are you heading up the coast again?

LYDIA: Yes, to my sister's beach house. It's not very flash, but we like it.

5 In your workbook, write a conversation between two people; for example, an argument, a confession, an interview or an interrogation. Your conversation must be accurately punctuated and include descriptions of how the characters speak. Include characteristics of real speech as appropriate. Perform your conversation with a partner.

Everyone knows the spelling rule '*i* before *e* except after *c*', but some people forget the second half of the rule and then they can't understand why there seem to be so many exceptions.

Look at the table below and try to work out the second half of the rule, then complete the sentence '*i* comes before *e* except when it's after *c*', as long as:

Group A		Group B		Group C	
ceiling	receipt	believe	field	eight	foreign
deceit		friend	siege	beige	height
receive		priest	achieve	neighbour	
conceited		grief		leisure	

Name: Due date: Guardian signature:

REVISION TEST 2

1 In each pair of sentences below, one sentence has an underlined clause. The other sentence has an underlined phrase. Tick the sentence in each pair in which the underlined part is a clause.

a i The new house on the corner has been empty for months. ______

ii The new house that has been built on the corner has been empty for months. ______

b i When you return home from school, you can help me with the garden. ______

ii On your return you can help me with the garden. ______

c i As there is a total fire ban today, we won't have a barbecue. ______

ii Because of the total fire ban, we won't have a barbecue. ______

d i After we finish the work on World War I, we will be studying the Great Depression. ______

ii After the work on World War I, we will be studying the Great Depression. ______

2 Identify the types of sentences as *simple*, *compound*, *complex* or *compound–complex*.

a I will cook dinner tonight. ______________________

b Because you will be late home, I will cook dinner tonight. ______________________

c I will do the shopping and then cook dinner tonight. ______________________

d I will do the shopping and then cook dinner tonight, because you will be home late.

____

3 Underline the predicate in these sentences.

a I will cook dinner tonight.

b After dinner we can watch a DVD.

c Our local shops close at six o'clock.

d Prices at the all-night convenience store are too expensive.

e Their labour costs are very high.

4 Add appropriate punctuation marks in the boxes.

Nissa gave Danny an unfriendly look. ☐ You heard what Lallie said ☐ Danny-O. He ☐ s with us. ☐

☐ Just like that? ☐ Danny demanded. 'We don ☐ t know anything about him. What if Lallie made a mistake ☐ '

☐ The choosing is over ☐ ' said Lallie dreamily ☐

A picture came into my mind of the way she had come up to me just outside the school ground and tagged me. Maybe it was some kind of game.

[ ] What do you mean the choosing [ ] Who chose me [ ] '

'No-one [ ] ' she answered [ ] looking momentarily less vague in her surprise. 'You chose to answer the Call.'

[ ] I didn [ ] t choose anything [ ] ' I said. My mother did all the choosing in my life for me I thought bitterly.

'We'd better get inside,' Nissa said briskly. She reached in her pocket and took out a set of keys [ ] holding them up to the green glow. For a moment her eyes caught mine, the keys dangling between us [ ]

Then she turned and slid the key into the library door [ ] pushing it open.

I gaped. How did Nissa come to have the library keys [ ]

Carmody, I 1993, *The Gathering*, Puffin Books, p. 44

5 Rewrite the words in the sentences below that need an apostrophe of possession or contraction.

a Dont you know? Youre supposed to meet them at St Patricks Square.

____

b If Id known, I wouldve cancelled the childrens party. ____________________

c Kerryns aunt and uncles Doberman has escaped. ____________________

d The Directors and Treasurers telephones have both been bugged.

____

e His father-in-laws travel guides were useful. ____________________

f Its not as simple as you think. ____________________

g When youve completed the test, compare your answers with Aynslies answers.

____

6 Explain the difference between *it's* and *its*.

____

____

7 Explain the difference between *who's* and *whose*.

____

____

Name: Due date: Guardian signature:

12 WORD ORIGINS, PREFIXES AND SUFFIXES

Vocabulary

Many words in English are derived and constructed from root words, prefixes and suffixes.

Simple **root words** and their meanings from Greek (Gk) and Latin (L.) form the basis of many English words. For example, the Greek root word *chrono* means 'time', and is the source of words such as *chronology* and *chronicle*. The Latin root word *finis* means 'end'. It appears in English words such as *final* and *finish*.

A **prefix** is a word component that is added to the beginning of a word to form or alter its meaning. Some common prefixes include:

anti– opposite

auto– self

bi– two

dis– not

mis– wrong

sub– under

pre– before

un– reverse

 *bi*lingual, *sub*marine, *pre*view

Prefixes also help to create antonyms (opposites) such as *misfortune*, *unnecessary* and *disobey*.

A **suffix** is a word component that is added to the end of a word to form a new meaning or to alter the word's part of speech. Common suffixes include:

–able to have ability

–ful complete

–ly possessing the quality

 accept*able*, use*ful*, slow*ly*

Write each English word in the list below with its root word and meaning in the table on the next page.

bicycle	monopoly	automatic	transport	unify
astrology	democracy	magnify	paragraph	thermometer
biology	centenary	microphone	telescope	metropolitan

There are many common prefixes and suffixes that are used to alter the meaning of words. Make sure you use the correct ones.

Root word	Meaning	Example from box
centum (L.)	one hundred	
unus (L.)	one	
magnus (L.)	large, great	
porto (L.)	to carry	
bi (L.)	two	
bios (Gk)	life	
demos (Gk)	people	
phone (Gk)	sound	

Root word	Meaning	Example from box
tele (Gk)	far	
auto (Gk)	self	
therme (Gk)	heat	
polis (Gk)	city	
grapho (Gk)	to write	
mono (Gk)	alone	
aster (Gk)	star	

1 Look up the meanings of the following Greek and Latin prefixes in a dictionary. In the space provided, write out the meaning of each prefix and then a word that contains that prefix. Then write a sentence for each word to show its meaning.

a *dia–* (Greek)

i Meaning: ____________________

ii Word that contains the prefix *dia–*: ____________________

iii Sentence: ____________________

____

b *hyper–* (Greek)

i Meaning: ____________________

ii Word that contains the prefix *hyper–*: ____________________

iii Sentence: ____________________

____

c *semi–* (Greek)

i Meaning: ____________________

ii Word that contains the prefix *semi–*: ____________________

iii Sentence: ____________________

____

d *para–* (Greek)

i Meaning: ____________________

ii Word that contains the prefix *para–*: ____________________

iii Sentence: ____________________

____

e *mal-* (Latin)

i Meaning: ______________________________

ii Word that contains the prefix *mal-*: ______________________________

iii Sentence: ______________________________

____

f *inter-* (Latin)

i Meaning: ______________________________

ii Word that contains the prefix *inter-*: ______________________________

iii Sentence: ______________________________

____

g *bene-* (Latin)

i Meaning: ______________________________

ii Word that contains the prefix *bene-*: ______________________________

iii Sentence: ______________________________

____

h *circum-* (Latin)

i Meaning: ______________________________

ii Word that contains the prefix *circum-*: ______________________________

iii Sentence: ______________________________

____

2 Make antonyms (opposites) out of the words below by adding either the prefix *dis-* (Latin for 'not') or *mis-* (Latin for 'wrong').

a ____________ appear
b ____________ lead
c ____________ rule
d ____________ adventure
e ____________ behave
f ____________ stress
g ____________ qualify
h ____________ trust
i ____________ spell
j ____________ understand
k ____________ loyal
l ____________ quiet

3 The table on page 52 lists some common suffixes and their meanings.

a Add to the table by writing three examples of words containing each suffix. (Use a dictionary to help you.) The first two have been done for you.

b Suffixes alter a word's part of speech. Using your dictionary, identify the part of speech of each word created by the additional suffix. Write the parts of speech in the table.

Suffix	Meaning	Examples	Part of speech
–ist	one who does	pianist, typist, artist	noun
–ship	skill	craftsmanship, entrepreneurship, leadership	noun
–less	without		
–er	one who is		
–ive	quality of		
–like	similar to		
–able	able to be		
–ion	action, process		

4 Using the suffixes listed above, make new words from those below and, for each one, identify the part of speech.

a companion ______________________

b hope ______________________

c femin ______________________

d laugh ______________________

e expedit ______________________

f paint ______________________

g creat ______________________

Can you work out the rule to explain why some of the words in the table below have dropped the *–e* when the suffix *–able* or *–ous* is added, and some have kept the *–e*? Clue: consider the position of vowels and consonants. Can you see patterns? Write your answer in the space below.

admire + able	admirable	advantage + ous	advantageous
adventure + ous	adventurous	approve + able	approvable
believe + able	believable	change + able	changeable
courage + ous	courageous	cure + able	curable
desire + able	desirable	dispense + able	dispensable
fame + ous	famous	grieve + ous	grievous
knowledge + able	knowledgeable	manage + able	manageable
marriage + able	marriageable	measure + able	measurable
move + able	movable	note + able	notable
notice + able	noticeable	pronounce + able	pronounceable
recognise + able	recognisable	service + able	serviceable
trace + able	traceable	value + able	valuable

____

____

____

Name: | Due date: | Guardian signature:

13 SYNONYMS, ANTONYMS AND HOMOPHONES

Vocabulary

A **synonym** is a word that has a similar meaning to another word. It can provide degrees of meaning. The ability to choose the best synonym can make your writing precise and sophisticated. The synonym of a word is always the same part of speech as the word it replaces.

happy (adjective) – cheerful, content, pleased

curl (verb) – bend, twist, entwine

An **antonym** is a word that has the opposite meaning to another word. Antonyms are sometimes formed by adding/changing prefixes or suffixes. The antonym of a word is also always the same part of speech as the word it replaces.

e.g. *scold* (verb) – approve, commend, praise

artificial (adjective) – authentic, genuine, natural

similar (adjective) – dissimilar, inconsistent, different

Homophones are words that sound the same, but are spelt differently and have different meanings.

- allowed/aloud
- alter/altar
- assent/ascent
- ate/eight
- by/bye/buy
- brake/break
- bored/board
- cereal/serial
- cite/sight/site
- check/cheque
- coarse/course
- counsel/council
- complement/compliment
- fair/fare
- foul/fowl
- hear/here
- hole/whole
- knew/new
- manner/manor
- missed/mist
- it's/its
- past/passed
- principal/principle
- pier/peer
- peace/piece
- practice/practise
- poor/pore/pour
- rite/right/write/wright
- rapt/wrapped
- sale/sail
- scene/seen
- stationary/stationery
- story/storey
- they're/their/there
- to/too/two
- threw/through
- whether/weather/wether
- weight/wait
- witch/which
- who's/whose
- you're/your

HAVE A GO

1 In the table of character vocabulary below, the first column contains keywords and the second column contains synonyms and antonyms of those words. Circle the two antonyms and underline the two synonyms for each keyword.

Keyword	Synonyms/Antonyms
humorous	solemn, comical, serious, amusing
competent	capable, proficient, ineffectual, inept
respectful	considerate, impolite, discourteous, well-mannered
courageous	cowardly, heroic, fearful, valiant

Keyword	Synonyms/Antonyms
admirable	praiseworthy, despicable, contemptible, commendable
gullible	clever, credulous, astute, naive
rebellious	defiant , compliant, obedient, disobedient
disloyal	traitorous, steadfast, trustworthy, unfaithful

The most common spelling errors in writing are caused by choosing the wrong homophone.

2 Cross out the incorrect word in the brackets so that the sentences make sense.

- **a** Athletes are reminded that trampoline (practice/practise) will be on Thursday morning at (ate/eight).
- **b** We (knew/new) that (piece/peace) had come at last.
- **c** Remember to (by/buy/bye) your (fare/fair) before boarding the train.
- **d** (Who's/Whose) house has more than one (storey/story)?
- **e** The (principle/principal) dancer was in every (scene/seen).

3 Write five sentences showing correct usage of homophones. Use the information at the beginning of this unit to help you.

TAKE IT FURTHER

1 Form antonyms by adding prefixes to the following words. Use the prefixes *dis–*, *il–*, *im–*, *in–*, *ir–*, *mis–* and *un–*.

- **a** ________adequate
- **b** ________legitimate
- **c** ________easy
- **d** ________responsible
- **e** ________proper
- **f** ________organised
- **g** ________understand
- **h** ________inform
- **i** ________appropriate
- **j** ________appoint
- **k** ________legible
- **l** ________regular
- **m** ________decided
- **n** ________modest
- **o** ________guided

2 Use the suffixes *-less* and *-ful* to create antonyms for the following words. Note: there is no double 'l' in *-ful* words.

a worthy ____________________
b tasty ____________________
c useless ____________________
d purposeless ____________________
e sensible ____________________
f thoughtful ____________________
g hopeful ____________________
h graceless ____________________
i powerless ____________________
j fearful ____________________
k cheerless ____________________
l fruitless ____________________
m hairy ____________________
n careless ____________________
o cluey ____________________

3 Rewrite the following letters to the editor and improve them by providing synonyms for the words in italics and selecting the correct homophones from the words in brackets.

a

Dear Editor,

Our city has been *hit* by a possum plague! Possums should not be (aloud/allowed) to *roam* freely in our suburbs. (They're/Their/There) presence is *unwelcome*. They have caused (grate/great) *damage* to our gardens by *eating* roses, fruit trees and *beautiful* camellias. Soon, Victoria will be the gardenless state! Not only do possums (brake/break) roof tiles with their (paws/pause), but they *ruin* ceilings with their droppings (too/to/two). The *smell* is (foul/fowl)!
(Its/It's) time the local (council/counsel) *solved* the possum problem!

Regards, Potty over possums

b

Dear Editor,

Why isn't more being done to clean up (our/hour) beaches? They are *filthy*! Yesterday the (weather/whether) was *lovely* so (eye/I) took my niece to the beach, but there was *rubbish* everywhere! We went (strait/straight) home! Our *wonderful* beaches are supposed (to/too) be the *best* in the world, but if local (councils/counsels) don't do (their/they're/there) part to make them look *presentable*, people will just *stop* going to the beach and visitors will stop coming (here/hear).

Regards, Disgruntled Beachgoer

4 **a** Find 10 synonyms for the word *say*.

b Write a conversation between at least two characters, using direct speech. Use synonyms for the verb *say* to describe how the characters speak. Remember to punctuate speech correctly (see Unit 11).

Revise all the homophones listed in this unit. In your next class, work with a partner and test each other on the list of homophones on page 53, as though you are in a spelling bee: say the word, spell out the word, give the word in a sentence and then repeat the word. Do five words each, and then swap. Test each other on at least 20 words.

Name: | Due date: | Guardian signature:

14 FIGURES OF SPEECH

Vocabulary

A **figure of speech** is an expression that suggests comparison between objects, and evokes images and ideas for the reader. There are three main figures of speech: similes, metaphors and personification.

A **simile** is a figure of speech in which one object is compared to another. The comparison is always made using the words *like* or *as*.

e.g. The wind was like a freight train.
The family gathering was as noisy as a circus.

A **metaphor** is a comparison in which one object is said to be or have the characteristics of another object.

e.g. The moon is a tarnished coin.
The lion has muscles of steel.

Personification involves attributing human qualities – both physical and psychological – to non-human beings and objects.

e.g. The trees waved their arms in distress.
The wind kicked the leaves along the alley.

1 Identify the following sentences as similes, metaphors and personifications by writing *S*, *M* or *P* as appropriate at the end of each sentence.

- **a** Thunder echoed like a bowling alley. ________
- **b** Rain raced through the streets and spat angrily on the windows. ________
- **c** Our car is a rocket, shooting along the freeway. ________
- **d** The moon is a ghost, peeping from the clouds. ________
- **e** It was as cold as a winter's day in Alaska. ________
- **f** All night the wind has muttered profanities at our doors and windows. ________
- **g** The flock of gulls is an airforce squadron, manoeuvring in unison across the sky. ________

2 English poet William Wordsworth's environmental appreciation poem 'I wandered lonely as a cloud' (1807) makes use of figures of speech.

I wandered lonely as a cloud

I wandered lonely as a cloud
That floats on high o'er vales and hills,
When all at once I saw a crowd,
A host of golden daffodils;
Beside the lake, beneath the trees,
Fluttering and dancing in the breeze.

Noticing how words are built from root words, with prefixes and suffixes added, can help you work out the meaning of unfamiliar words.

Continuous as the stars that shine
And twinkle on the milky way,
They stretched in never-ending line
Along the margins of the bay:
Ten thousand saw I at a glance,
Tossing their heads in sprightly dance.

The waves beside them danced: but they
Outdid the sparkling waves in glee;
A poet could not but be gay,
In such a jocund company;
I gazed – and gazed – but little thought
What wealth the show to me had brought.

For oft, when on my couch I lie
In vacant or in pensive mood,
They flash upon that inward eye
Which is the bliss of solitude;
And then my heart with pleasure fills,
And dances with the daffodils.

Wordsworth, W 1807, 'I wondered lonely as a cloud'.

a Underline the similes in Wordsworth's poem.

b The daffodils are personified in an extended figure of speech that runs through most of the poem. What does Wordsworth liken the daffodils to?

c What else dances in the poem?

3 Many poems begin with similes, metaphors and personification. With a partner, locate a poetry anthology. Find examples of similes, metaphors and personifications in the poems. Create a poster of examples of similes, metaphors and personifications. Remember to give the title and author of each poem you use as an example. Alternatively, you could prepare a slide presentation of your examples for the class.

4 Write a metaphor for each element.

eg. fire: Fires are savage beasts, gobbling up the bushland.

a earth: ____________________

b air: ____________________

c fire: ____________________

d water: ____________________

5 Make up similes for the following phrases.

- **a** as happy as ____________________
- **b** as angry as ____________________
- **c** as bright as ____________________
- **d** as gloomy as ____________________
- **e** as tall as ____________________
- **f** as short as ____________________
- **g** as loud as ____________________
- **h** as quiet as ____________________
- **i** as funny as ____________________
- **j** as serious as ____________________

TAKE IT FURTHER

Clichés are 'tired', overworked expressions. Many of them were originally examples of the use of figurative language and were probably quite original and interesting the first few times they were used.

e.g. Your suggestion went down like a lead balloon. (simile)
As far as I'm concerned, he is sandwich short of a picnic. (metaphor)

1 Figurative expressions that have become clichés are drawn from a wide range of contexts. Match the list of contexts with the examples below.

Ancient warfare	Lighting, before the days of electricity
Blacksmithing	Mining
Card playing	Naval term
Horseriding	Undertaking

- **a** We will need *all hands on deck* to ensure that the school musical is a great success.
- **b** We must *strike while the iron is hot.*
- **c** Those who *live by the sword die by the sword.*
- **d** Her comment was just *another nail in the coffin.*
- **e** We've *hit pay dirt!*
- **f** She's *holding all the cards.*
- **g** I know that you feel nervous after the accident but it is important to *get back in the saddle.*

h You can't keep *burning the candle at both ends.*

2 Identify whether the following clichés are examples of *similes* or *metaphors*.

a You have *egg on your face* because of that gaffe. ____________

b Her refusal just confirms that she has a *heart of stone*. ____________

c She's *buzzing like a bee* with excitement. ____________

d You're too late; you've *missed the boat*. ____________

e They don't appreciate what she has to offer; she feels that she is *hitting her head against a brick wall*. ____________

f I'm as poor *as a church mouse*. ____________

3 In the pairs of sentences below, one sentence is literally true and the other is an example of figurative language. Underline the sentences that are figurative.

a i His forehead was clouded with anger.

ii The sky was clouded.

b i He leapt over the last hurdle and won the race.

ii There are many hurdles that must be faced in life.

c i The police wrung a confession from the subject.

ii We wrung out the washing.

d i The mouse creeps into the hole.

ii Time creeps by when you are bored.

e i The old car is rusty.

ii My memory of algebra is rather rusty.

f i The lifesaver rescued the drowning man.

ii The debater was drowning in his own words.

g i The crowd flew through the gate.

ii The bird flew over the gate.

The following words are part of the metalanguage of English – that is, the words we use when writing or talking about English as a subject. Make sure that you can spell them all. In your next class, work with a partner to test each other.

Practise any words that you can't spell in whatever way helps you most to remember the spelling of a word: use the look-cover-spell-check method; write the word several times; close your eyes and visualise the word as you spell it aloud; or write the word and highlight the part of the word that gives you trouble.

anthology	literary	personification	rhythm	writer
comparison	literature	poetry	simile	written
imagery	metaphor	rhyme	verse	

Name: | Due date: | Guardian signature:

15 LANGUAGE REGISTER – INFORMAL LANGUAGE

Vocabulary

Language register refers to the words and style used by the writer to achieve a purpose and engage an audience. Language registers can be either formal or informal. A formal language register observes conventional standard grammar and vocabulary. An informal language register is like the language and vocabulary used in everyday speech, or more casual situations. In this unit, the focus is on informal language registers.

Colloquial language is informal, everyday, conversational language that includes idioms and slang. Swear words are an unacceptable form of colloquial language. Colloquial language incorporates contractions such as *I'll*, *haven't* and *doesn't*, as well as abbreviations such as *fridge* and TV. Generally, colloquial language is not grammatically correct. For instance, you will often hear people say *could of* instead of the grammatically correct *could have*. Colloquial language is best used informally; it can undermine formal speech and writing.

A major aspect of colloquial language is the use of **idioms** – common words and expressions particular to a specific country. Some well-known Australian idioms that are part of our everyday, informal language include *fair dinkum*, *she'll be right* and *mad as a cut snake*.

Slang is highly informal colloquial language. Often, slang conveys negative connotations and can be offensive. It is not considered standard English, although it is used widely. Slang (such as teenage slang or criminal slang) often identifies a group and it is constantly changing.

feral, yuppie, true-that, devo, whatevs, tomoz, wannabe

Jargon is specialised language and terminology associated with a particular occupation or field of study. It can be highly technical, such as some engineering, legal and bureaucratic terminology. Most new jargon currently is generated in computer technology.

gigs, cloud, interface, hyperlink

1 Beside each word below is a list of synonyms. Underline the slang term among the synonyms for each word. Then write two of your own current slang terms for each word.

a lazy: idle, inactive, bludge, slothful, slack

b idiot: fool, airhead, simpleton, cretin, imbecile

c curious: inquisitive, enquiring, questioning, stickybeak, prying

d frightened: afraid, spooked, petrified, alarmed, horrified

The most important question to ask when making choices about language register is: 'What is appropriate for the purpose, the context and the audience?'

e proud: conceited, arrogant, self-important, vain, bigheaded

f shy: bashful, backward, hesitant, modest, coy

2 In the table below, some common Australian idioms and their meanings have been jumbled. Match the idioms with their meanings by writing the letter of the idiom (a–o) next to its corresponding meaning.

	Idiom	Meaning	
a	to bark up the wrong tree	to be an unconventional family member	
b	to beat about the bush	to make an attempt	
c	to be led up the garden path	to lose one's temper	
d	to let the cat out of the bag	to brush away flies	
e	to put one's best foot forward	to have a tantrum	
f	to be the black sheep of the family	to be mistaken	
g	to not know whether one is Arthur or Martha	to exaggerate one's achievements	
h	to give the Aussie salute	to be unimpressive, low quality	
i	to give it a burl/bash	to succeed, to be given a chance	
j	to big-note oneself	to reveal a secret	
k	to go off one's block	to be unclear, indirect	
l	to be the first cab off the rank	to be confused	
m	to be not much chop	to try one's hardest	
n	to spit the dummy	to be the first to do something	
o	to get a guernsey	to be misled, tricked or deceived	

3 Electronic information technology and social media jargon and slang are widespread in our society. Make a list of at least five terms used in relation to electronic information technology or social media.

4 Browse through your Science, History or Maths textbooks. Make a list of 10 subject-specific words and write their meanings. You could present this to the class as a slide presentation.

1 Australian slang incorporates some colourful (and occasionally unflattering) terms to describe animals, people and human qualities. Who, or what, are the following?

Who/What	Answer	Who/What	Answer
ankle-biter		banana bender	
earbasher		duffer	
dobber		ocker	
pommy		battler	
bitser		chalkie	
Joe Blake		larrikin	

2 Make a list of five current slang expressions in use at your school. Give the meaning of each expression. Avoid offending anyone in your school community.

Slang expression	Meaning

3 Rewrite the following paragraph in plain language, making its meaning clear.

This warranty does not extend to accessories or defects or injuries caused by or resulting from causes not attributable to faulty parts or the manufacture of the product, including but not limited to, defect or injury caused by or resulting from misuse, abuse, neglect, accidental damage, improper voltage, liquid spillage, vermin infestation, software, use of consumables other than those approved by The Company, or any alterations made to the product that are not authorised by The Company.

4 In your workbook, write a response to the letter below, outlining your view about slang. Give three reasons and some examples to support your view.

Dear Editor

Our English language is being ruined by the infiltration of slang. Slang is vulgar and offensive! It is overused and boring! A slang word is 'in' one day, and 'out' the next, making language meaningless and imprecise. People use slang inappropriately – even our politicians have stooped so low as to bandy derogatory slang expressions in parliament. Ban slang now!

Mr Green, ACT

SPELLING FOCUS The following words appear in this unit. Add a tick next to the ones that are spelt correctly and a cross next to the ones that are spelt incorrectly. Write the correct spelling in the space next to the words spelt incorrectly.

convensional	[ ]		conversasional	[ ]	
abbreviations	[ ]		collochial	[ ]	
conotasions	[ ]		specialised	[ ]	
terminology	[ ]		bureaucratic	[ ]	

Name: | Due date: | Guardian signature:

16 NON-DISCRIMINATORY AND EMOTIVE LANGUAGE

Vocabulary

Language can be offensive when it expresses prejudice against people on the basis of their gender, race, age, disability, culture, socioeconomic status or sexuality.

Discriminatory language presents negative and judgemental stereotypes of people. There are several ways in which language can be discriminatory:

→ invisibility/exclusion

e.g. Mankind has been responsible for some remarkable inventions.

→ stereotyped descriptions of people

e.g. Participants in the Mardi Gras minced and pranced down Oxford Street.

→ unnecessarily focusing on a person's racial background to perpetuate negative images

e.g. Five students, only one of whom was Caucasian, were suspended.

→ language that insults or degrades people.

e.g. They were acting like a pack of old ladies.

Some terms for discriminatory language include: sexist (on the basis of gender), racist (on the basis of race), classist/elitist (on the basis of socioeconomic standing), ageist (on the basis of age) and heterosexist/homophobic (on the basis of sexuality).

Emotive words are used extensively in persuasive writing and speaking to convince others of an author's point of view on a controversial issue.

Emotive words express bias, a tendency towards a particular point of view or preference.

There are three types of emotive words:

→ positive words, which express approval and give a favourable impression, as well as suggesting the 'good' aspects

→ negative words, which express disapproval and give an unfavourable opinion, as well as suggesting the 'bad' aspects

→ neutral words, which are impartial and do not express bias.

e.g. *Celebrity* could be considered neutral; *dignitary* could be considered positive; and *big-wig* could be considered negative.

Chance could be neutral; *opportunity* could be positive; and *risk* could be negative.

1 Discriminatory language often creates unfavourable stereotypes of people. What is a stereotype? Circle the letter for the correct dictionary meaning of 'stereotype'.

a *n.* all those qualities that make a person, group or thing what he, she or it is, and how it is different from others

b *n.* a fixed general image or a set of characteristics that a lot of people believe represent a particular type of person or thing

c *n.* an individual human being

Collins Cobuild Advanced Learner's English Dictionary (5th edn, 2006) p. 1419.

Discriminatory language excludes people. Aim to make language choices that are inclusive.

2 From the list below, choose the non-discriminatory terms that match the discriminatory terms in the first column of the table. Write them in the second column. In the third column, explain why the term in the first column is discriminatory: is it on the basis of *gender, age, class, sexuality, race* or *disability*?

Irish person	Indigenous people	sales assistant	humankind	homosexual
financially disadvantaged	chairperson	senior citizens	cleaner	manager
intellectually impaired	Anglo-Australian	young people	constructed	visually impaired
		sportsperson	paraplegic/ quadriplegic	

Discriminatory term	Non-discriminatory term	Explanation
Natives		
salesman		
the old folk		
mankind		
sportsman		
Paddy		
the blind		
manageress		
queer		
chairman		
juveniles		
convict		
retard		
cleaning lady		
man-made		
the plebs		
cripple		

3 Reorganise these thesaurus entries into the correct categories in the table that follows.

- → confidence: assurance, boldness, courage, nerve, certainty, self-reliance
- → destroy: demolish, bulldoze, dismantle, pulverise, exterminate, smash
- → slim: lean, skinny, slender, thin, trim, slight
- → juvenile: babyish, immature, inexperienced, undeveloped, young, childish
- → nostalgia: homesickness, longing, regret, remembrance, yearning, wistfulness

Keyword	Neutral words	Positive emotive words	Negative emotive words
confidence			
destroy			

Keyword	Neutral words	Positive emotive words	Negative emotive words
slim			
juvenile			
nostalgia			

TAKE IT FURTHER

1 Rewrite the sentences and alter the pronouns *he*, *his* and *him* to make the sentences inclusive. You might be able to rewrite some of the sentences in more than one of the following ways:

- → Rewrite the sentence in the plural.
- → Leave out the pronoun (see Unit 2).
- → Use *he or she, she or he* or *s/he.*
- → Use other pronouns such as *you, I, we* or *one.*
- → Use *they, them* or *their* as singular pronouns.

a The average Australian employee works eight hours a day; therefore, he will work 40 hours per week.

b Before entering the exam room, each student should check his desk number and ensure that he has writing materials.

c The applicant is advised to bring his résumé to the interview.

2 Write these synonyms for 'old' in the correct column in the table that follows.

advanced in years	elderly	in one's dotage	senile
aged	full of years	mature	third age
ancient	getting on	over the hill	
decrepit	grey-haired	past one's prime	

Discriminatory	Non-discriminatory

3 Give the following crime news report an appropriate neutral tone by replacing the words in italics with words of similar meaning from the list below.

laughing	shouted	busy	requested
entered	reaching	forced	take
held	pointed	ran	

An attendant was *captured* at gunpoint and *compelled* to hand over cash at a *bustling* inner-Sydney petrol station. Police said the thief *raided* the petrol station at 10 o'clock on Friday morning. He *screamed* at the attendant, *demanded* money and *poked* a sawn-off shot-gun at him before *lunging* over to *grab* money from the cash register. The attendant told police that the thief *scurried* out the door *cackling* to himself.

SPELLING FOCUS

Here are some words to do with discriminatory or emotive language. Make sure that you can spell them all. In your next class, work with a partner to test each other.

ageist	exclusion	judgement	racial
discriminatory	gender	persuasive	stereotype
emotive	heterosexual	prejudice	stereotypical

Name: | Due date: | Guardian signature:

17 THE LANGUAGE OF IMAGINATIVE TEXTS

Vocabulary

Texts can be broadly classified as:

→ imaginative
→ informative
→ persuasive (or argumentative).

Different types of texts use different structures and different language features. It is helpful to know the conventions, even if the decision is sometimes made to break away from what is expected.

Many texts have features of more than one type of text. For example, a persuasive text aimed at convincing young people not to take up smoking might include excerpts from a report (an informative text); and a recipe book consisting mainly of procedural texts giving instructions might include passages of recount, in which the recipe writer remembers the significance of particular recipes in his or her family background.

Imaginative text types include:

→ narrative fiction (novels, short stories)
→ literary descriptions
→ recounts
→ play and film scripts
→ poems and verse novels.

There are conventions about the structure and language features of imaginative texts. For example, most narratives follow a conventional structure with a clear beginning, middle and end. Play and film scripts are written according to conventional formats.

In most imaginative texts the emotive connotations of words are significant.

1 Narrative texts include many different structural conventions. Draw a line to match each convention in the first column with its meaning in the second column.

Column A	Column B
resolution	the highest point of the action
complication	an optional comment or moral
climax	the opening, asking 'who?', 'where?' and 'when?'
coda	the ending where the threads of the narrative are brought together
orientation	a problem or difficulty

Imaginative text types include fictional narratives and literary descriptions.

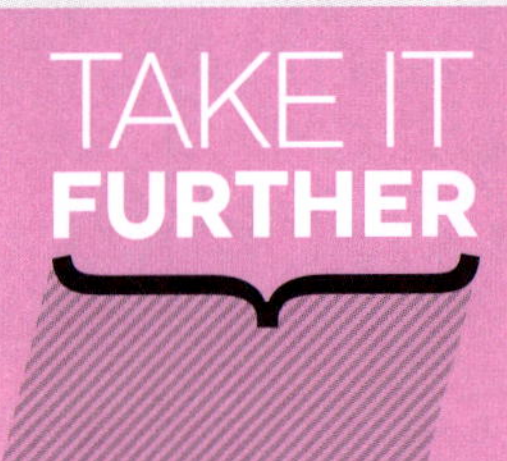

Narratives usually belong to particular genres, such as fantasy, science fiction, thriller or romance. Different genres have their own conventions. While some authors experiment with subverting the conventions, subversion only works because readers and viewers know what to expect – and know when those expectations are overturned. For example, a science-fiction novel might reveal on the last page that the characters with whom the reader has empathised are in fact aliens.

1 What are some of the features or conventions that you would expect in each of the following narrative genres?

a Romance

b Science-fiction

c Fantasy

d Thriller

Some narratives are metafiction. Metafiction deliberately draws attention to the fact that it is fiction. This can be done in different ways; e.g. providing alternative endings to a novel, making it clear that there is no 'correct' ending, as an ending is something the author shapes. In films an actor might suddenly step out of character and address viewers directly – reminding us that we are watching an actor acting, not a real story.

2 Write two examples of metafiction that you have come across – in print or on screen.

Here are some of the words used in this unit. Make sure that you can spell them.

imaginative	complication	narrative
literary	resolution	genre
orientation	connotation	metafiction

Name: | Due date: | Guardian signature:

18 THE LANGUAGE OF INFORMATIVE TEXTS

Vocabulary

Informative text types include:

- → factual descriptions
- → factual recounts
- → explanations
- → procedures
- → reports.

The purpose of informative texts is obviously to provide information. To do this well, texts need to be properly organised, usually with an introduction that sets out clearly the purpose of the text. Informative texts use factual, non-emotive language; vocabulary is often precise and can be technical.

Read the following text.

I made a terrific chocolate cake the other day. A bit crumbly and rather rich, but very yummy. I melted some dark chocolate – you know, over a bowl of boiling water. I beat up some butter, brown sugar and vanilla – I used my new electric beaters, which are great because they make the mixture all light and fluffy. Then I threw in three eggs – one at a time – and poured in the chocolate. Oh, I made sure that the chocolate had cooled first. Then I added some self-raising flour mixed with cocoa. I had to sift them together first. Actually, I added about half the flour mixture, quite gently – I think they say 'folding' rather than 'mixing' – and some milk. When that was combined I folded in the rest of the flour and a bit more milk. I then poured it all into a pan. Oh, I forgot to say that you need to grease the pan and line it with baking paper, otherwise the cake will stick. You cook it in the oven for about 40 to 45 minutes. Of course, you need to turn the oven on before you start, so it's hot when you are ready to put the cake in to cook. It was really good. You should try it!

1 This text is enthusiastic but not very informative. What are its faults as a procedural text?

2 Rewrite the recipe as a procedural text, numbering the steps, putting the processes in the correct order, and using the command form of the verbs ('fold', 'beat', 'mix').
The ingredients have been listed and the first step has been done for you.

You will need: 200 g chopped dark chocolate, 200 g softened butter, 1 cup brown sugar, 1 teaspoon vanilla extract, 3 eggs, 1½ cups self-raising flour, 2 tablespoons cocoa, ½ cup milk.

1 Preheat oven to 170°C. Grease and line the base of a deep, round cake tin (6 cm × 22 cm).

Good informative texts use very precise language, including technical language where required.

TAKE IT FURTHER

The following description is an example of an imaginative text. It is a literary description, using emotive words and expressing a personal opinion. Read the text, noting the use of emotive words.

Katinka is a Siamese cat. She is absolutely beautiful – I just love her brilliantly blue eyes that are like almonds. She's two years old now but she's still as playful as a kitten – that's one of the characteristics of the breed. They love people. Katinka hates it when I leave for school each morning. She cries almost like a baby – Siamese cats have a very distinctive miaow and she knows that I can't resist her when she begs for something. She's not very big but she has a long, slim body and an elegant neck. She has a dear little pointy-shaped nose, like a triangle. That suits her because she's very inquisitive, constantly sticking her nose into everything. She's a lovely creamy sort of colour and like all Siamese she has darker hair on her face, her ears and her toes. Her coat's quite short and very soft, and of course she loves being stroked.

Rewrite the text as a factual text, describing the Siamese cat breed using the information about the appearance of the cats, their voices and their behaviour.

SPELLING FOCUS

Here are some words that relate to the content of this unit. Make sure that you can spell them.

procedural	process	explanation	exposition
proceed	explain	explanatory	expository

Name: | Due date: | Guardian signature:

19 THE LANGUAGE OF PERSUASIVE TEXTS

Vocabulary

Persuasive or argumentative texts range from texts that simply set out different points of view in a calm and balanced fashion to propaganda that uses all kinds of persuasive tricks to sway the opinions of readers, listeners or viewers.

Argumentative or persuasive texts include:

→ a written discussion of an issue
→ a speech in a debate
→ an advertisement
→ a political speech
→ an editorial
→ a letter to a newspaper editor
→ a blog expressing a point of view or arguing a case.

In assessing an argument or persuasive text, consider:

→ the choice of words (emotive or factual?)
→ the use of evidence (Is it reliable? Can it be verified?)
→ the use of rhetorical devices such as repetition and questions
→ the implied relationship between writer/speaker and audience.

When writing or composing argumentative or persuasive texts, the speaker or writer can use the tool of modality. **Modal words** express the level of certainty about a point that is being made. They can add different shades of meaning to a text.

e.g. He *can* write the letter. vs He *should* write the letter.

Another popular technique in persuasive writing or speaking is the use of **rhetorical questions** – that is, questions to which no answer is expected or where only one answer is really possible.

e.g. Do we really want logging of rainforests to continue? (in a letter to the editor opposing logging)
Do we want a bankrupt economy? (in a political speech)

1 Explain why each passage could be considered a persuasive text.

a From a political speech: The opposition does not understand public welfare in this country. Statistics show an alarming rate of poverty, which is increasing. My friends, do we want more Australians living in poverty? Should we cut welfare funding?

b From a newspaper editorial: The state of our roads is appalling and the latest announcement by the government to decrease funding for the improvement of country roads is disgusting. The government should be utterly ashamed. Hundreds of people died last year on our roads. Hundreds. How many more need to die for this to change?

Well-chosen emotive language can add power to persuasive texts.

2 In each of the examples below, the modal verbs or nouns are italicised. In each set of examples, rank them from most intense (1) to least intense (3).

a i The government *must* repeal this legislation immediately. ________

ii The government *can* repeal this legislation immediately. ________

iii The government *should* repeal this legislation immediately. ________

b i There is a *possibility* of severe drought in this region as a result of climate change. ________

ii There is a *probability* of severe drought in this region as a result of climate change. ________

iii There is a *certainty* of severe drought in this region as a result of climate change. ________

c i A strict school uniform *ought to* improve the tone of a school. ________

ii A strict school uniform *can* improve the tone of a school. ________

iii A strict school uniform *must* improve the tone of a school. ________

TAKE IT FURTHER

Make up a rhetorical question that you could include in an essay or speech on each of the following topics.

a young people and driving

b climate change

c compulsory school exams

SPELLING FOCUS

The following words are all related to the content of this unit. Make sure that you can spell them.

altercation	contention	disagreement	exhortation	propaganda
conflict	controversy	dispute	promotion	squabble

Name: Due date: Guardian signature:

Vocabulary

REVISION TEST 3

1 Indicate whether the following are similes (S), metaphors (M) or personification (P) by writing the correct letter in the box at the end of each sentence.

a The angry waves threw themselves onto the rocks. [ ]

b That chair is like a royal throne. [ ]

c Our house was as hot as a pizza oven. [ ]

d The zoo is a dismal prison. [ ]

e The washing machine huffs and puffs its way through the cycle, gasping for enough energy to get the job done. [ ]

f Since the students left for summer holidays, the school has been a cemetery. [ ]

g The moon was so pale it was like a ghost. [ ]

h The vintage car groaned into life and ambled slowly out of the driveway. [ ]

i The trees are windmills on the horizon. [ ]

2 Underline the colloquial and slang terms in these sentences and give their meanings.

a As an ankle-biter, he was given to spitting the dummy when he couldn't get his way.

____

b We told Grandma to stop beating about the bush, so she let the cat out of the bag.

____

____

c Mum advised me to put my best foot forward and give the paper round a bash.

____

d My aunt – who is a Banana bender – is regarded as the black sheep of the family.

____

____

e Suzie went off her block when she saw what we'd done to her garden. I agreed that it wasn't much chop.

____

____

3 Explain why each of the following statements is discriminatory.

a Primitive natives once roamed this desert.

b 'That's just so gay!' laughed Brent, refusing to read the class novel.

c Like all Chinese, Lee is great at maths but uncomfortable with more creative subjects such as drama.

d 'She can't be a very good mechanic,' said Lucy. 'I mean, she's a woman!'

e The football team played like a pack of old ladies.

4 Alter the following sentences so that they are inclusive.

a Mankind is considered the most dangerous animal on Earth because of his ability to think.

b Each contestant should ensure he has the right equipment and has synchronised his watch.

c I have an appointment with the lady doctor.

d The male nurse gave me the injection.

5 Write the words in the list in the appropriate columns in the table that follows.

accustomed	established	fuddy-duddy	old-fashioned
conventional	fixed	historic	time-honoured
customary	folk	long-established	

Neutral	Positive	Negative

Name: Due date: Guardian signature:

20 PARAGRAPHS

Paragraphs and essays

Paragraphs usually consist of several sentences arranged in a logical way to develop and explain a main idea.

→ The main idea is stated in a single sentence – the **topic sentence**. Generally, the topic sentence is the first sentence of the paragraph; however, it can be effectively placed elsewhere in the paragraph. Also, a topic sentence can take the form of a question.

→ Other sentences explain and illustrate the main idea: they are the **explanatory sentences**. A sentence that does not contribute to the main idea should not be included – it is an **irrelevant sentence**.

→ Explanations and examples in paragraphs are logically organised and linked using conjunctions or other linking words and phrases, including prepositions and relative pronouns.

→ A paragraph finishes with either a **concluding sentence**, which summarises the main idea; or a **linking sentence**, which leads to the next paragraph in an essay.

Paragraphs range in length according to their purpose. Generally, they contain from 25 to 250 words; or one to 10 sentences. The modern trend is towards shorter paragraphs. Here is a list of notes that a senior student made in order to write a paragraph about ways to reduce the road toll.

{ Driver education programs; stricter penalties on road law-breakers; better roads and cars; pedestrians and cyclists should observe road laws; drivers shouldn't drink-drive }

Here is the final paragraph:

Topic sentence

Australians must implement several ways to reduce the tragic road toll. The government should enforce stricter penalties on drivers *who* break road laws, particularly concerning speeding and drink-driving. *Obviously*, the current penalties are not working *and* need to be increased to deter drivers. *Also*, money should be spent on keeping roads in good condition – especially country roads and highways *that* have been the site of horrific accidents. Cars should be maintained in good mechanical order *and* regularly inspected for road worthiness and safety through spot-checks by the police. *In addition*, drivers should be more careful about observing road laws *and* refrain from driving when drunk by organising a designated driver *who* will avoid alcohol and drugs. *Furthermore*, the government could organise road-law and driver-education programs for all students. The road toll would also be reduced *if* pedestrians behaved responsibly by observing the road laws and avoiding jay-walking. Cyclists would fare better *if* they wore helmets *and* used lights and reflectors at night. These are some practical ways in *which* all Australians can help to reduce the road toll.

Sample explanatory sentence – reason and example

Relative pronouns, used to link clauses

Other linking words, used to link sentences

Sample explanatory sentence – reason and example

Concluding sentence

Conjunctions, used to link clauses

Paragraphs must have a topic sentence

The three extracts below are from Year 9 and Year 10 History, Home Economics and Biology textbooks. Identify the parts of a paragraph in each one by:

- underlining the topic sentence
- drawing a wavy line under the explanatory sentences
- circling conjunctions or other linking words or phrases
- drawing a dotted line under the concluding sentence
- crossing out any irrelevant sentences.

EXTRACT A

The Renaissance began in Italy due to a number of factors. First, Italy had been the centre of the Roman Empire, and all over the country monuments provided a reminder of Rome's past greatness, as well as inspiration for a revival of classical culture. At this time, English peasants were struggling under the feudal system. A second reason was that in Italy there were many independent cities in which lived a large middle class, as well as a professional class. These cities were expanding economically, and had an active social and intellectual life. Consequently, Italy was ready for the Renaissance.

EXTRACT B

Healthiness can be achieved by following a few guidelines. Obviously, fresh air and water are essential ingredients for the human body to function well. Regular exercise encourages physical fitness and endurance. A balanced diet, which includes consumption of the basic food groups and avoids excessive indulgence in sugars, fats and drugs, will promote good health. There is a good, affordable range of foods in supermarkets. In addition, people need a positive attitude and an interest and enthusiasm in life, without which we would lose our willpower to either exercise or eat properly. Basically, healthiness is a balance of air, water, exercise, diet and positive attitude.

EXTRACT C

How does a tadpole develop into a frog? One frog can lay more than a thousand tiny eggs. The eggs, which are always laid in water, are surrounded by a jelly to protect them as there are many predators living in and around the water. Soon, small tadpoles develop from the eggs in the water. Within three weeks, they develop a mouth, eyes and gills. Also, they grow a much longer tail, enabling them to swim. When their tail completely disappears, lungs replace the gills. As the tadpoles continue to grow, two small back legs eventually appear. These back legs grow larger and more powerful, while small front legs grow at the same time. The tadpoles have become small frogs, able to jump high into the air.

1 'Odd spot' is an anecdote describing an unsual or humorous news story. In the following 'odd spot' paragraphs, the sentences are out of order. Write each group of sentences in the correct order to achieve clarity of meaning.

a

The bears also tucked into marshmallows and honey. A mother bear broke into a holiday cabin in Norway with her three cubs, downed 100 cans of beer and trashed the furniture. 'They had a party in there,' said the cabin's owner, Even Borthen Nilsen.

The Age, 13 August 2012

b

The cobra wasn't so lucky; it died of its injuries. Mohamed Salmo Miya had been working in his rice paddy when the serpent attacked. 'I bit it with my teeth because I was angry,' the 55-year-old said. A Nepali man was bitten by a cobra and bit it back. He was treated at a village health post and is in no danger.

The Age, 24 August 2012

2 Using the notes that follow, write a one-paragraph news report of youth complaints made at a Carltonborough council meeting about the lack of activities for youth in the area. Create a clear topic sentence and use conjunctions or other linking words/phrases to achieve a fluent news report.

- teenagers complained of the lack of activities and services for them in Carltonborough
- no social youth group or drop-in centre
- no sporting associations for teenagers between the ages of 12 and 18
- the library has limited technological resources and opening hours
- fitness circuits, cricket pitch and oval in disrepair and dangerous to use
- general lack of sports facilities in the area
- increased admission cost to public swimming pool
- the bus service to the city terminates at 10 p.m. on Fridays and Saturdays
- there is no youth worker or counsellor in the area
- there is a reduced number of part-time jobs since the Superfood market closed
- apart from Carltonborough High School, there are no alternative educational courses for teenagers wishing to learn specialised subjects, trades and professions

3 In your workbook, write a paragraph on one of the following topics. Use the example on page 77 to develop and write your paragraph. First, make a list of relevant points to include in your paragraph, then organise your points into a logical order. Write a topic sentence, the explanation sentences, and finally the concluding sentence. Use conjunctions to achieve fluency.

Topics:

- → I need to get a part-time job.
- → Sport is an important part of my life.
- → Australia can be improved in many ways.
- → The person I most admire is ...
- → How to be a good friend.
- → My favourite weekend activity is ...

SPELLING FOCUS

The following words can be difficult to spell. Add a tick next to the ones that are spelt correctly and a cross next to the ones that are spelt incorrectly. Write the correct spelling in the space next to the words spelt incorrectly.

Word		Correct spelling	Word		Correct spelling
explainatory	[✗]		irrelevant	[ ]	
terminates	[ ]		inspirasion	[✗]	
indipendant	[✗]		professional	[ ]	
intellectual	[ ]		indulgence	[ ]	
venimouse	[✗]		worthyness	[✗]	

Name:

Due date:

Guardian signature:

21 PREPARING TO WRITE AN ESSAY

Paragraphs and essays

Unpacking and understanding an essay topic is essential to preparing an effective essay. There are three steps to unpacking an essay topic.

1 IDENTIFYING ESSAY TOPIC TERMS

The two basic types of essay topics are expository and analytical.

Expository essay topics require an explanation of a subject. They can often be identified by the inclusion of the following keywords:

→ define: give the precise meaning of the subject
→ account for: give reasons or causes for something (*Why?*, *What?* or *How?* are often used)
→ describe: give detailed factual information about the subject
→ summarise/outline/state: give the main features of the subject
→ explain: point out the significance of something
→ illustrate: give concrete, specific examples, figures and diagrams to clarify the subject.

Essay topic: 'Account for the use of symbolism in Chaucer's writing.'

Analytical essay topics require a thoughtful and critical response to a subject. They incorporate the following keywords:

→ discuss: consider all aspects of the subject (arguments for/against, reasons)
→ evaluate: consider the value and/or effectiveness of the subject
→ compare/contrast: give similarities and differences
→ justify: give reasons to support an argument or point of view on the subject
→ question: give a supported answer (*Do you agree*? or *To what extent …?* is often used)
→ criticise: give supported judgements on the subject.

Essay topic: 'Compare and contrast the use of humour in *The Curious Incident of the Dog in the Night-time* and *Flowers for Algernon*.'

2 KEY WORDS AND PARAPHRASING

Give definitions of **keywords**, **phrases** and **terms** (italics in the example below) used in the topic to clarify your understanding. Look up synonyms for the keywords. Using this list of synonyms, write a simple paraphrase (in your own words) of the topic to clarify it in your mind. You can use this paraphrase in your essay.

Essay topic: '*Great Expectations* shows the *dangers* of allowing *obsession* and *revenge* to *control* one's life.' Discuss.

Paraphrase: *Great Expectations* portrays the hazards of letting personal fixations and grudges influence one's life.

3 'THE QUESTION ASKS ME TO …'

Complete this sentence to help you clarify what you have to do in order to write a relevant response to the topic.

(based on *Great Expectations* above) The question asks me to talk about how obsession and revenge have a dangerous effect on the characters in the novel.

It is essential to identify keywords in an essay question.

1 Identify the following essay topics as expository (E) or analytical (A).

a Summer or winter: which season do you prefer? ______
b Write a biographical description of a significant Australian historical figure. ______
c 'The mass media are irresponsible.' Discuss. ______
d What are the advantages of owning a pet? ______
e 'Honesty is the best policy.' What do you think? ______
f Is the federal government's approach to reducing youth unemployment working? ______
g Write a report illustrating the food chain. ______
h 'Good literature must have heroic characters.' Discuss. ______
i Explain the rules of basketball. ______
j Present arguments for and against changing the Australian national anthem. ______

2 For each subject listed, write two essay topics: one expository and one analytical.

a Australia should be a republic.

i Expository:

ii Analytical:

b School hours should be from 10 a.m. to 4.30 p.m.

i Expository:

ii Analytical:

c Lowering taxes in Australia

i Expository:

ii Analytical:

3 Below you will find three essay topics on *To Kill a Mockingbird*, by Harper Lee. The keywords in each essay topic are in bold. Select two synonyms from the list for each keyword.

disappointment	instructed	gloomy	growth	negative
positive	realise	encounters	adventures	understand
progress	hopeful	informed	letdown	

a 'Both as a father and lawyer, Atticus Finch is a **failure**.' Do you agree?

b Do you think *To Kill a Mockingbird* is an **optimistic** or a **pessimistic** novel?

c 'Children **learn** more from their personal **experiences** than they do by simply being **told** about something.' Discuss with reference to the **development** of Scout and Jem in *To Kill a Mockingbird*.

4 Using the list of synonyms in exercise 2, write a paraphrase of each essay topic in exercise 3.

TAKE IT FURTHER

1 Select an essay topic from 'Have a go' exercise 1 on page 82. Complete the following to assist you in unpacking the topic. Write your essay in your workbook. Alternatively, you could choose an essay topic based on the novel you are currently studying or on a topic provided by your teacher.

Essay topic: ______________________________

____

Type of essay topic: expository or analytical? ______________________________

Keywords: ______________________________

____

Synonyms for keywords (give three for each): ______________________________

____

____

Paraphrase of topic using synonyms: ______________________________

____

____

The question asks me to talk about: ______________________________

____

____

2 Choose one of the following essay topics and unpack it using the method in exercise 1.

→ Illustrate the ways in which you might increase your pocket money.
→ Honesty or dishonesty – which do you think is better?
→ Compare and contrast your best and worst holidays.
→ 'Teenagers should have an evening curfew of 9 p.m.' Do you agree or disagree?

Essay topic: ______________________________

____

Type of essay topic: expository or analytical? ______________________________

Keywords: ______________________________

____

Synonyms for keywords (give three for each): ______________________________

____

____

Paraphrase of topic using synonyms: ______________________________

____

____

The question asks me to talk about: ______________________________

____

____

SPELLING FOCUS

The following words appear in this unit. Add a tick next to the ones that are spelt correctly and a cross next to the ones that are spelt incorrectly. Write the correct spelling in the space next to the words spelt incorrectly.

relevent	[ ]	________	inclusion	[ ]	________
expository	[ ]	________	criticle	[ ]	________
annaliticle	[ ]	________	significance	[ ]	________
judgements	[ ]	________	ilastrate	[ ]	________

Name: | Due date: | Guardian signature:

22 PLANNING AN ESSAY

Paragraphs and essays

Planning enables you to develop an organised, detailed, effective and relevant essay. A lack of planning could result in an unconvincing and confusing essay that strays from the topic and does not address the question.

Three ways of planning an essay:

1 OUTLINE FORMAT

This includes key ideas; their supporting points and evidence to support these points; and sequential numbering of the points (1, 2, 3 for main points; a, b, c for supporting points; i, ii, iii for evidence or sub-points of supporting points).

2 BOX CHART FORMAT

This consists of three columns: key factor, supporting points and evidence.

3 DIAGRAM FORMAT

This includes a central box (or circle) containing the topic; three or four branches leading from the central box to boxes containing supporting points; and further branches leading from these to boxes containing evidence.

In order to present a clear and convincing response, you must have a point of view on the topic. Some possible points of view include:

→ agreement with the topic: *Yes*
→ disagreement with the topic: *No*
→ a qualified response where you agree or disagree to a certain point: *Yes, but* … or *No, but* … or *No, however* ….

The essay plans below represent a response to this topic:

'Outline the factors that may lead teenagers to take up a life of crime.'

Identify each type of essay plan format. (Write 'outline', 'box chart' or 'diagram' on the line provided.)

a

Key factor	Supporting points	Evidence
Family problems	Lack of communication Conflict Unstable home life	Increased rate of family break-ups
Media influence	Portrayal of violence and crime as glamorous Ready information about committing crimes Poor media role models	Refer to a violent film and media crime figure Internet 'how-to' crime guides

Good essays involve careful planning.

Key factor	Supporting points	Evidence
Negative personal feelings	Sense of failure and hopelessness Frustration and anger Lack of ambition Limited skills Giving in to peer pressure Boredom	Refer to the youth unemployment, school drop-out/homelessness rates

This essay plan is an example of the ______________ format.

b

1 Family problems
   - a Lack of communication
   - b Conflict
   - c Unstable home life
     Increased rate of family break-ups

2 Media influence
   - a Violence and crime portrayed as glamorous
     Refer to a violent film
   - b Poor media role models
     Refer to media crime figure
   - c Ready information about committing crimes
     Internet 'how-to' crime guides

3 Negative personal feelings
   - a Sense of failure and hopelessness; frustration and anger; lack of ambition; limited skills; boredom
     Refer to youth unemployment, school drop-out, homelessness rates
   - b Giving in to peer pressure

This essay plan is an example of the ______________ format.

c

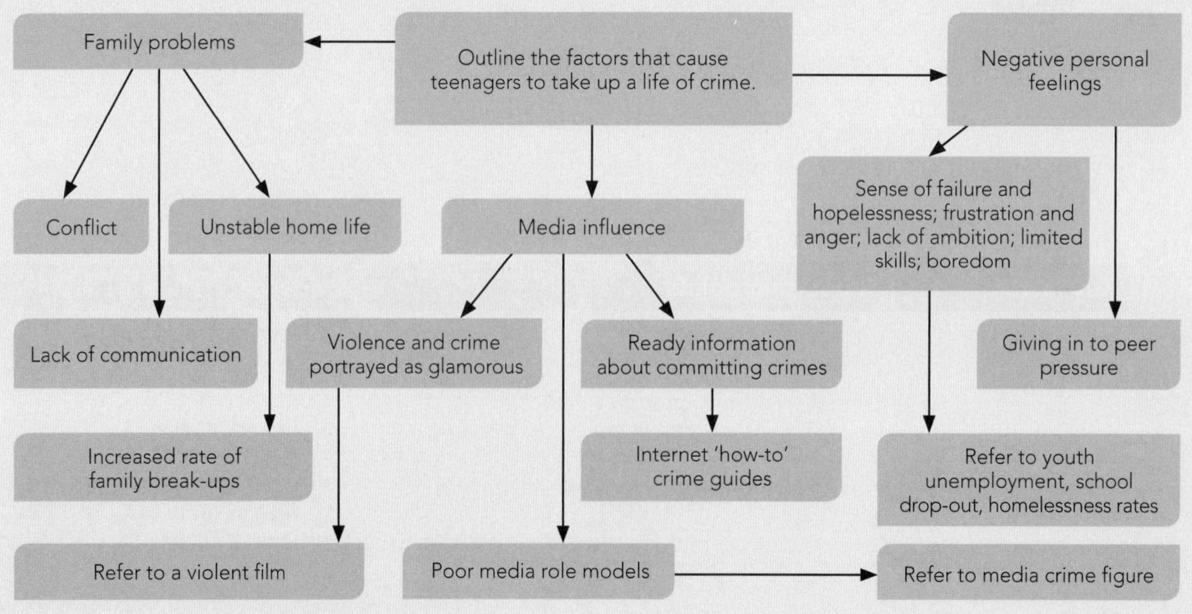

This essay plan is an example of the ______________ format.

2 With a partner, list the benefits and limitations of each type of plan. Which type of plan do you prefer? Why?

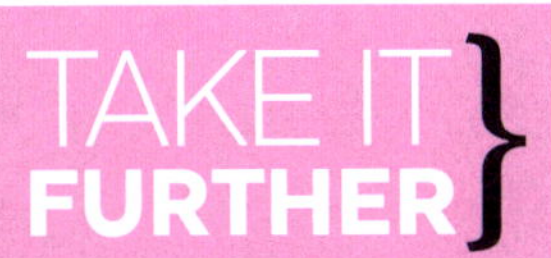

Read the essay below.

The ideal pet

Mice are perfect pets. They combine the best features of popular small house pets such as cats, some dog breeds and guinea pigs. Mice are fun, cheap and adaptable pets.

Mice are entertaining and affectionate pets. They are busy and playful, offering hours of amusing observation as they scurry, dig and play chasey in their cages. Mice are intelligent and can be taught tricks such as negotiating a maze by using simple rewards and punishments. They are attractive and cute pets because they have a range of colours and produce different types of fur. As mice are tame, they are usually not dangerous; therefore, they're suitable for young children and you don't have to display a 'Beware of savage mouse' sign on your front gate! Furthermore, they are social animals and enjoy human company – they love being petted and being carried around in pockets.

Generally, mice are inexpensive and easy to care for. Apart from the initial expenses, such as buying the mice as well as a cage and basic cage equipment, mice are fairly cheap to keep. You can recycle newspapers by shredding them and using them as cage liners or bedding. Also, mice will eat fruit, vegetable and table scraps, as well as stale biscuits and bread. Although keeping mice requires responsibility for their care, veterinary treatment for sick mice is simple and affordable, unlike the exaggerated bills for cats and dogs. In order to avoid odours, cages need to be cleaned out regularly; however, you don't need to wash, clip or groom mice. Despite popular opinion, mice are very clean and spend hours washing and grooming themselves.

Importantly, mice are adaptable to any human lifestyle. As they occupy a small space by requiring only a cage, mice are ideal for apartments and small houses. Mice are easily transported in their cages and you can even take them on holidays instead of paying for boarding or an animal-sitter. Besides, they're quiet. Have you ever heard of a mouse barking at the moon?

It's easy to understand why mice are the number-one house pet in Singapore. Mice provide people with amusement and affection, and they're affordable and manageable.

Reconstruct what might have been the essay plan, using the following box chart diagram.

Key factor	Supporting points	Evidence

SPELLING FOCUS

1 Use the word list below to complete the exercises.

bough	thorough	tough	thought
through	cough	though	fought

a In the word *drought*, the 'ough' makes the same sound as in one of the words in the word list above. Which word is this?

b In the list above, there is a word in which the 'ough' makes the same sound as in *enough*. Which word is this?

c In the list above, find two words that rhyme and write them here.

2 Make sure you can spell all the words in exercise 1 correctly. In your next class, work with a partner and test each other.

Name: Due date: Guardian signature:

23 WRITING A GENERAL ESSAY

Paragraphs and essays

Generally, the 'five-paragraph essay structure' is the most common way of writing an essay. This format has an introductory paragraph, three body paragraphs and a concluding paragraph.

INTRODUCTORY PARAGRAPH

An effective **introductory paragraph** captures the reader's attention and includes a statement clarifying the subject or the point of view that will be expressed. Some ways to begin an essay include:

- → paraphrase – a statement of the topic in your own words
- → anecdote – a brief descriptive story illustrating the subject or point of view
- → quotation – statements by relevant experts, famous writers or celebrities illustrating the subject or point of view
- → statistic – a powerful figure illustrating the subject or point of view
- → question/answer – ask a question of the subject and respond with a brief answer illustrating the subject or point of view
- → historical/background context – a brief description of the who, what and where, illustrating the subject or point of view.

BODY PARAGRAPHS

Body paragraphs expand the content presented in the introduction (see Unit 20 for basic paragraph structure). These paragraphs can be developed by adding examples, facts and figures, definitions, key vocabulary/terms, descriptions of processes, and explanations of causes and their effects.

CONCLUDING PARAGRAPH

Concluding paragraphs can include:

- → summary phrases – *In summary …, In review …, Overall …*
- → recommendations – offering solutions, options or alternatives on the subject
- → cautions – warnings of the consequences of a subject if particular action is not taken
- → quotations – statements by relevant experts, famous writers or other notable people summarising the essay
- → prediction – a suggestion of what might happen in the future.

INFORMATIVE ESSAYS

There are different types of essays. The most common type of essay required in most subjects is the **informative essay**. An informative essay uses the common five-paragraph essay structure and communicates the essential facts about a topic or issue. Facts are observable, measurable and demonstrable realities. They are often presented as evidence and information. There are different types of facts that can be incorporated into an informative essay:

- → definitions – explanations of meaning from dictionaries or specialist research texts
- → personal experience – a person's direct experience, knowledge and observations
- → examples and anecdotes – illustrations of an idea
- → statistics, surveys – numerical data showing the frequency of a phenomenon or 'sample opinion' on an issue
- → visual evidence – photographs, film footage and other graphics (for example, a cartoon) illustrating an idea.

Good essays contain informative detail.

Read the first-draft essay below about the potential causes of juvenile delinquency.

First-draft essay

[1] Did you know that the offending rate for teenagers aged 15 to 19 is three times that of all other offenders? Juvenile delinquency is law-breaking by people under 18 years of age, and has many possible causes. However, are all teenagers who break the law juvenile delinquents? Juvenile delinquents could be split into two groups. The first group includes occasional under-age law-breakers. The second group includes teenagers who commit crimes regularly. Juvenile crime is on the increase in our society. The occurrence of juvenile delinquency could be attributed to a lack of communication in families, influence from violent films and television, the media, alcohol and drugs.

[2] Lack of communication in families could be considered one of the first factors that could lead to juvenile delinquency. If teenagers have no one to speak with in the family about their problems, they may turn to other ways of coping, such as using alcohol and drugs. When a family doesn't communicate well, teenagers may not receive the attention and care they need to develop into well-adjusted human beings. They may find themselves so desperate for attention that they will do something outrageous such as committing a crime, which will be guaranteed to get a reaction – hopefully that of attention and care from adults. Lack of communication can also cause teenagers to 'bottle up' their emotions until they no longer find it possible to stay in control. By the time they reach this point, they may be so full of anger and frustration that they may do something drastic. One student, angry about his parents' busy lifestyle, 'trashed' the family home!

[3] Alcohol and drugs are other factors that can lead to under-age law-breaking. It is illegal for any person under the age of 18 to purchase or consume alcohol (unless with a parent or guardian). When under the influence of alcohol teenagers can experience a variety of negative reactions. These can range from violence to extreme depression. Some suddenly feel very courageous; they feel 'untouchable' and as though they have found a way to escape their problems. Reality can become distorted. Drunken teenagers can lose control of themselves, and the situations they find themselves in may involve law-breaking, including public brawling, stealing and vandalism. Using drugs such as ice, ecstasy, marijuana, heroin and cocaine can ultimately lead to criminal behaviour: with increasing dependence comes the need to support the habit by dealing and stealing. The desperation that drug addiction produces may even lead to homelessness and prostitution.

[4] Forms of media – television, films, books, advertising, the Internet and computer games – distort reality and present crime and violence as common and acceptable. Media can desensitise people by constantly presenting stereotyped ideas, negative role models, and gratuitous sex and violence. In recent years, it has become obvious that violent media images can have negative effects on teenage audiences. Teenagers mimic the behaviour of media role models by copying their actions and adopting their ideas. If their hero can get away with doing wrong and harming others, why can't they do so themselves? In many films, the 'good guy' is the one who blows off the head of his enemy! Often no consequences are shown and very little emotion is displayed. Sometimes violence and crime are shown in hilarious ways. Humans are made to look disposable. Many of the recent violent gang rapes and club killings in Sydney and Melbourne have been linked to blockbuster films in their style of crime.

[5] These are the main potential causes of juvenile delinquency – a lack of communication in families, alcohol and drug abuse and violent media images. When teenagers are exposed to one or more of these factors, they may soon find themselves in trouble with the law.

1 List the features of the introduction.

2 List the features of the conclusion.

3 The essay lacks informative detail. Match each item of information from the following table with the paragraph of the essay in which it would best fit. (Write the paragraph number in the table.)

Informative detail	Paragraph Number
Social worker Dr Budd said that the increase in juvenile crime was due to the increased incidence of family breakdowns in our society.	
In a recent case, a teenage gang attacked a 15-year-old with a machete for the leather jacket he was wearing.	
In the previous decade, juveniles were responsible for 5% of homicides, 10% of serious assaults, 20% of robberies, 12% of rapes, 28% of burglaries, 33% of thefts and 27% of vehicle thefts.	
Like the vast majority of young offenders, Jonno's background is one of disrupted family life and a series of foster homes.	
Juvenile delinquents – particularly repeat offenders – were often wary, aggressive, angry, resentful and unpredictable, a police spokesperson confirmed.	
The president of Victims of Crime blamed the increasing violence that children are exposed to on television and in films for the trend towards more violent juvenile crime.	
According to those working with juvenile offenders, alcohol and illegal amphetamines are increasingly linked to crimes.	
'Parents are neglecting their responsibility to listen to and guide their children,' said a senior Children's Court magistrate.	
The Police Commissioner has expressed concern over the recent spate of books by convicted violent criminals that glorify the criminal lifestyle and provide 'instruction manuals' for committing crimes.	

TAKE IT FURTHER

1 In your workbook, rewrite the essay on page 90 to give it substance, incorporating the additional information that was supplied in 'Have a go' exercise 3.

2 Once you have written your essay, refer to the checklists at the start of Unit 27 (page 105) to ensure that you have fulfilled the requirements of writing an effective essay.
How could you improve your essay?

SPELLING FOCUS

Many of the words that are part of the metalanguage of the subject English are notoriously difficult to spell. Each word below has one or more letters missing – the number of letters missing corresponds to the number of spaces. Rewrite the words, filling in the missing letter or letters.

a acron_m
b adjectiv_l
c al_iteration
d anon_mous
e anteced_nt
f asson_nce
g cari_ature
h gloss_ry
i gra_ _atical
j lit_ _ature
k onomatop_ _ia
l person_fication
m play_right
n pr_judice
o _seudonym
p repe_ _tion
q rh_me
r rh_thm
s solilo_ _y
t sp_ _ker
u sp_ _ch
v t_ _tology

Name: Due date: Guardian signature:

24 WRITING A PERSUASIVE ESSAY

Paragraphs and essays

The purpose of a **persuasive essay** is to convince others of your point of view on an issue or text. Persuasive essays are commonly written in response to analytical essay topics.

Generally, a persuasive essay is organised in the common five-paragraph essay format. However, as well as paraphrasing the essay topic and defining keywords, a persuasive essay also contains a point of view (a contention or assertion) in the introduction. The body paragraphs of the persuasive essay contain reasons and evidence to support the point of view. The concluding paragraph then reinforces the point of view or argument.

Some persuasive essays include a paragraph exploring the opposing point of view that is being presented in the essay. This is often followed by a paragraph explaining why the opposing point of view is not valid, and allows the writer to supply further evidence or arguments towards their own point of view. If the writer is able to discredit the opposing point of view, the writer's own argument appears more valid. It is also a way to acknowledge that the writer has considered the opposing points of view, making the writer's argument appear fair and objective.

An effective persuasive essay contains a range of persuasive-language techniques and content:

- → figures of speech
- → emotive language
- → emphasis – repetition (of keywords, names); cumulation (repeating words of similar meaning); alliteration (repetition of the first letter)
- → facts – personal experience (a person's direct experience, knowledge and observations); definitions (explanations of meaning); examples; statistics or surveys (numerical data showing frequency of a phenomenon or 'sample opinion' on an issue)
- → experts – individuals (or organisations) who have detailed knowledge and skill in the particular subject.

1 Identify the persuasive-language technique being used in each statement.

a Survey results reveal that 97 per cent of people are in favour of the proposal.

b It is an abysmal, abhorrent and atrocious proposal.

2 Write each of the persuasive-language features from the list below next to the appropriate paragraphs of the essay on the next page. Some annotations have been completed for you.

Negative language
Fact – personal experience
Statistic
Negative language
Emphasis – cumulation, alliteration
Fact – personal experience
Positive language
Fact – scientific
Statistic
Fact – example
Figurative language – metaphor
Point of view
Example
Quoting of expert
Emotive language
Statistic
Positive language

A persuasive essay uses a variety of language techniques to argue a point of view.

Figurative language – metaphor

Positive language

Point of view

Statistic

Quoting of expert

Emotive language

Example

Essay topic: 'The environment – preservation or devastation?' Discuss.

Australia is a toxic rubbish tip! Many factors that have a significant impact on Australia's devastating environmental problems – including water wastage, air pollution and waste production – can easily be managed if all Australians adopt a greener lifestyle.

As one of the driest continents, Australia's water resources are extremely limited – the usage of water is a critical, urgent and serious national issue. Currently, we are experiencing drought conditions. However, 50% of Australian households don't take any measures to conserve water! Every year, Australian households consume approximately 1.829 gigalitres of water – the equivalent of 1.829 billion Olympic-sized swimming pools! Too many people naively and selfishly think water will always flow out of their taps because they pay for it. We must change our attitudes to preserve this vital resource.

A few sensible, simple and straightforward steps can help reduce our daily water wastage at home. Wastage can be minimised by ensuring that taps are always turned off properly and don't leak. My parents were embarrassed by the amount of water dripped by our leaking shower – 3.5 litres in one day! Shorter showers and setting the dishwasher on 'economy wash' are essential steps. Using the 'grey water' from the final rinse/spin cycle of the washing machine to water the garden and wash the car will not only save water, but also reduce water bills. With a bit of effort and organisation, Australian households can reduce water wastage.

In a recent survey (Australian Bureau of Statistics), 68% of people reported environmental concerns about air pollution and the damaging effects on air quality. Motor vehicle emissions create the most serious air pollutants in terms of human health and environmental impact. Some fumes stay in the atmosphere for up to 16 years – degrading the air and causing respiratory problems. Although Australian cities are regularly covered with thick brown smog, 71% of Australians use cars every day and only 16% use public transport on weekdays.

Australians can take responsibility for air pollution by making sure car exhaust systems are in good working condition. Using public transport and bikes where possible may take some personal reorganisation, but car usage, and therefore fumes, would be reduced. On weekdays, sharing a single car with other commuters would help ease traffic congestion and lower air pollution.

1 Write the final body paragraph of the essay (i.e. not the conclusion) on the previous page. The focus of this paragraph is 'household and commercial business waste production' and some solutions for reducing waste. Use the following research in your paragraph, as well as your own ideas. Use the checklist to ensure you achieve correct paragraph structure and include a range of persuasive techniques.

Research

- → Australia is the second-highest producer of waste behind the USA.
- → Australians produce 20 million tonnes of rubbish per year.
- → The amount of waste placed in tips (landfill) per year is enough to cover the entire surface of Victoria to a depth of 10 cm.
- → Many tips are nearing full capacity.
- → Effects on environment – waterways pollution, injuring/killing wildlife, dangerous greenhouse gases, visual pollution
- → Recycle – glass, plastic, paper/cardboard
- → Reuse – paper, containers
- → Avoid plastic bags and excessive packaging.
- → Visit the Australian Bureau of Statistics website for facts and figures about waste and the environment: www.abs.com.au.
- → Visit the Clean Up Australia website for facts and figures about waste and the environment: www.cleanup.com.au.

Paragraph checklist

- → Topic sentence
- → Use of a figure of speech
- → Use of emotive language
- → Use of different types of facts
- → Use of an expert
- → Use of emphasis
- → Concluding sentence

2 Here is the concluding paragraph to the essay.

> The community must stop exploiting the environment for personal, social and economic benefits. Once an area of wilderness is destroyed, once a natural resource is depleted, it is impossible to replace it – it is lost forever! If we wish to preserve the environment for the health and enjoyment of future generations, we must take action now! Society can either choose to take responsibility for Australia's current problems and take measures to prevent further deterioration, or society can allow the current destruction and wastage to continue.

a How is repetition used for emphasis in this concluding paragraph?

b Does the conclusion reinforce the point of view of the essay?

SPELLING FOCUS

A lot of words belonging to the metalanguage of the subject English appear in this unit. Make sure that you can spell all the words in the following list. In your next class, work with a partner and test each other.

alliteration	emphasis	persuasive
argument	evidence	phenomenon
conclusion	explanation	rebutting
cumulation	introduction	repetition
definition	paragraph	statistic
emotive	persuasion	technique

Name: | Due date: | Guardian signature:

25 WRITING A TEXT-RESPONSE ESSAY

Paragraphs and essays

A **text-response essay** presents a critical interpretation of a text in response to a topic. Generally, a text response is written using the common five-paragraph essay structure. It is essential to unpack a text-response topic and to research and plan your response before writing.

Ten tips for writing a text-response essay:

1. Know the text in detail – reread or review the text.
2. Understand the requirements of the topic – spend time 'unpacking' the topic.
3. Research and plan your response.
4. Present a point of view on the topic – outline your point of view in the introduction.
5. Give reasons for your point of view – present one reason per paragraph.
6. Give evidence for your point of view – explain specific details from the text in response to the question; provide relevant quotations.
7. Vary your vocabulary – use accurate synonyms for key topic words; use specific vocabulary to discuss characters, themes, and so on.
8. Punctuate titles correctly – underline, quotation marks or italics.
9. Spell titles, character names and author names correctly.
10. Put quotations from the text in quotation marks.

Five tips for layout in a text-response essay:

1. Write page or chapter numbers in brackets after quotes.

e.g. 'It is hard for the free fish to understand what is happening to the hooked one.' (7)

2. Incorporate short quotations in your response by enclosing them in quotation marks. If the quotation does not flow naturally in the sentence, it should be introduced with a comma or colon.

e.g. Reuven, now a young man, is angered and frustrated by the imposed silence between himself and Danny: 'Silence was ugly, it was black, it leered, it was cancerous, it was death. I hated it.' (230)

3. Incorporate long quotations in your response by introducing them with a colon, setting them out on a new line and enclosing them with quotation marks.

e.g. Reb Saunders, Danny's father, discloses that he has enforced silence on his son because he is anxious about his son's intelligence. Reb Saunders explains:

> 'How will I teach his mind to have a soul? How will I teach his mind to understand pain? How will I teach it to want to take on another person's suffering?' (276)

4. Incorporate specific references to the text without quoting directly by paraphrasing.

e.g. Reb Saunders agonises about how to teach his son's mind to have a soul.

5. Use an ellipsis (three dots only) to indicate where words or phrases have been omitted from a quote.

e.g. Danny's internal conflict is powerfully described in a vivid image: 'A spider had spun a web … there was a housefly trapped in it now … The fly's tiny black legs flayed the air fiercely, then its wings were free again, buzzing noisily, but its body remained glued fast …' (173–4).

Source of quotes in examples: Chaim Potok 1986, *The Chosen*, Penguin, pp. 7, 173–4, 230, 276.

Be sure to unpack the question as the first step in planning a text-response essay.

Here is a first-draft essay on the topic: 'In *Great Expectations* both Pip and Estella are the victims of the manipulations and self-centredness of others, with disastrous results. Discuss.'

Read the essay and complete the following tasks.

[1] Dickens' *Great Expectations* is set during the post-industrial revolution in England and explores the consequences of Pip's excessive ambition to become a 'gentleman'. During the novel, Pip adopts the materialistic and social values of upper-class London and foregoes his background, relationships and true self with devastating personal results. In *Great Expectations*, Pip and Estella are controlled and used by selfish characters and both suffer harmful consequences. However, Pip manages to regain control of his life while Estella remains a victim, although she gains some awareness that she has been manipulated.

[2] Since her adoption, Estella's life has been totally influenced by Miss Havisham. Miss Havisham used Estella as a tool to take revenge on males since she was jilted at the altar. She moulded Estella into a superior and sophisticated woman, whom she uses to bait men's interest and admiration only to have them disappointed by Estella's emotional coldness. Throughout the novel, Estella slowly begins to realise what her life has become and despises the fact that she has no control over it: 'Miss Havisham would have me wait, and not marry yet; but I am tired of the life I have led … and I am willing enough to change it.' (157) Although she tries to rebel against Miss Havisham by marrying the uncouth Bentley Drummle, Estella becomes self-destructive and regretful about what has happened to her. Meanwhile, she remains a heartless woman since Miss Havisham 'stole her heart away and put ice in its place' (132). Towards the end of the novel, Estella's awareness of having been manipulated is shown in her final conversation with Pip; however, she remains an innocent victim.

[3] Miss Havisham not only controls Estella's life, but she also influences Pip's values and mind. Her efforts to exploit Pip for her own self-interest cause him some negative experiences. After Pip's first visit to Satis House he is inspired to become a gentleman and is hypnotised by Estella's beauty. Miss Havisham takes advantage of Pip by encouraging his interests further. When Pip receives the news of a secret benefactor, he immediately assumes it is Miss Havisham. Although she is not his benefactor, she does not discourage his belief when he tells her of this, showing his gratitude. Pip is further manipulated by Miss Havisham when she places a 'love curse' (260) on him: 'Hear me, Pip! I adopted her to be loved. I bred her and educated her to be loved. I developed her into what she is, that she might be loved. Love her!' (263) Through Miss Havisham's deceptions and misleading interactions, Pip was led to believe that Miss Havisham was his benefactor and that Estella was meant for him in marriage. However, when the falseness of these ideas became clear, Pip is devastated and humiliated. Pip realises that 'Miss Havisham's intentions towards me, all a mere dream; Estella not designed for me …' (420).

[4] Magwitch used Pip to create the gentleman he had always wanted to be. Pip was moulded by Magwitch to become a compassionate gentleman. Magwitch shows fatherly affection towards Pip as a proud creator does on seeing his 'successful creation' (320). Once Magwitch reveals that he is the benefactor, Pip is shattered and decides that he cannot accept the criminal's money any longer.

[5] Estella's 'infectious' ridicule of Pip – 'He calls the knaves Jacks, this boy! … And what coarse hands he has. And what thick boots!' (90) – is all she has to do to manipulate Pip into wanting to become the gentleman she could admire and marry. In striving to become the perfect gentleman, Pip turns against those who brought him up. However, Estella leads Pip on, but withholds her feelings from him throughout the novel. When Pip learns that she does not love him, his heart is broken and he understands that he has been cruelly manipulated for the benefit of others.

[6] Arrogant and self-important characters manipulate both Pip and Estella into becoming self-centred people similar to themselves. Although Pip is controlled by Miss Havisham, Magwitch and Estella, he manages to find the ability to overcome them. Although Estella gains awareness of being controlled, she is still a pawn, unable to change.

1 Write a paraphrase of the student's point of view on the topic as stated in the introductory paragraph (paragraph 1).

2 Write synonyms for the keywords *victims*, *manipulations*, *self-centredness* and *disastrous* that are used in the essay.

3 The text title has been italicised throughout. What is an alternative way of punctuating the text title?

4 Write an example of a topic sentence from the essay.

5 Write an example of a direct quotation from the essay.

6 Why is an ellipsis used in paragraph 2?

7 Why is it important to include quotes from the text when writing a text-response essay?

1 Complete the following tasks by referring to the essay in 'Have a go'.

a Paragraphs 4 and 5 are brief and lacking in detail. Refer to the list of tips outlined on page 97 for writing a text-response essay and make some suggestions as to how these paragraphs could be developed further.

b The conclusion is weak because it is similar to the introduction. Rewrite the conclusion so that it summarises the key points.

SPELLING FOCUS

The following words appear throughout this unit. Add a tick next to the ones that are spelt correctly and a cross next to the ones that are spelt incorrectly. Write the correct spelling in the space next to the words spelt incorrectly.

criticical	[ ]		character	[ ]	
interpretation	[ ]		recquirement	[ ]	
punctuate	[ ]		disasterous	[ ]	
incorprorate	[ ]		sophisticated	[ ]	
quotation	[ ]		revolution	[ ]	
specific	[ ]		menipulate	[ ]	
ommitted	[ ]		gratitude	[ ]	
paraphraise	[ ]		ellipsis	[ ]	
compassionate	[ ]		benifactor	[ ]	
excessive	[ ]		disclose	[ ]	

Name: Due date: Guardian signature:

26 WRITING A REPORT

Paragraphs and essays

A report provides information on a topic. It usually consists of:

→ an introductory paragraph
→ a series of paragraphs about the topic, each one looking at a different aspect
→ a concluding paragraph that summarises the findings of the report.

Most reports are written in the present tense, although past tense is appropriate if writing a report on a historical topic. It is acceptable to include topic headings for each section (paragraph) of a report. Text connectives (such as conjunctions, adverbs and adverbial phrases) are used to link sentences and paragraphs. For example, a report on an event such as a sports carnival might use connectives to do with time: *at the beginning of the day*, *after the assembly*, *firstly*, *secondly*, *then* and so on. A report on an issue might use connectives such as *however* and *on the other hand*.

1 The first step in preparing a report is to collect the information. List reliable sources of information that could be used to gather notes for a report.

2 Why do you need to be careful if you are using websites as sources of information?

3 Below are some student notes for a four-paragraph informative essay about the fruit-bat problems in Australian cities. Organise the notes into the appropriate paragraph topics in the table on the next page.

Orchard pest
Hendra virus first identified in 1994
Relocate bats to an appropriate environment
Migratory – travel along east coast of Australia
Hendra virus possibly spread to horses by bats
Damage plants, trees and gardens
Endangered species
Cull the bats
Population explosion in city botanic gardens – especially during breeding season
Grey-headed flying foxes
Threat to rare plants in botanic gardens
Eat – eucalypt nectar, fruit, leaves
Hendra virus can be fatal to humans
Bat droppings destroy lawn and ground plants

Reports need a clear, logical structure.

Deter them with noise at night

No evidence that Hendra virus is spread directly to humans by bats

Noisy and smelly

Paragraph 1: definition of bats	
Paragraph 2: problems	
Paragraph 3: possible specific threat	
Paragraph 4: solutions	

TAKE IT FURTHER

Use the notes from the table in 'Have a go' exercise 3 to write the four-paragraph essay in the space provided. Include clear topic sentences and use conjunctions or link words/phrases to achieve fluency.

1 Nominalisation (changing verbs into nouns) is used frequently in reports, especially academic reports. Write the noun that can be formed from each of the verbs below, taking care with the spelling.

Verb	Noun
contend	
propose	
discuss	
repeat	
apply	
persuade	
collude	
recognise	
explain	
justify	
summarise	

2 Everyone learns differently. It is important to know which techniques of learning work best for you. Think about spelling: which methods help you most? Do you use the look-say-cover-spell-check method? Do you like to close your eyes and visualise the word? Do you need to write it down before you know whether it is correct? If a word gives you trouble, do you learn it best by spelling it in your head, by writing and rewriting it many times or by highlighting the difficult parts – perhaps using highlighter pens or different fonts on the computer? Does it help to have a list of your special spelling words taped on the wall above your desk? Does it help to make a rule to learn a few words every day?

Talk to a partner about the methods that work best for you. Then write a paragraph summarising those methods.

Name: | Due date: | Guardian signature:

27 EDITING AND PROOFREADING AN ESSAY OR REPORT

Use the following checklist to ensure that your essay is effective.

GENERAL EDITING AND PROOFREADING CHECKLIST

Content

- → Have I answered the essay topic question or addressed the report topic?
- → Is the content relevant?
- → Do I provide evidence to support my subject or point of view?

Structure

- → Have I included an introduction and a conclusion?
- → Do the body paragraphs contain a topic sentence, elaboration and a concluding sentence?
- → Is each paragraph organised in logical order?

Mechanics

- → Is the spelling accurate?
- → Is the vocabulary appropriate to the subject, audience and purpose?
- → Is the punctuation accurate and consistent?
- → Are sentences clearly expressed (complete sentences, subject–verb agreement, consistent tense)?

Read the following text-response essay and complete the tasks. As you read, you will notice that the essay paragraphs are out of order. They are labelled (A–F), so that you will be able to refer to them in the tasks that follow.

Topic: 'Outline the development of Macbeth's ambition'

[A] Very early in the play, Macbeth's developing sense of purposeful ambition is obvious. After hearing the witches' prophecies about his future as a king, he contemplates: 'If chance will have me King, why chance may crown me, / Without my stir'. This suggests not only that Macbeth is wondering how he will become king, but also that he has enthusiastically accepted as fact that he will actually be king. At this initial stage, he relies on the power of 'chance' to crown him – he would rather not 'stir'. Macbeth would rather become king as a result of fate, or chance circumstances.

[B] Finally, Macbeth acknowledges his intense ambition. In a later speech, he again emphasises the idea of taking some action to become king: 'I have no spur / To prick the sides of my intent, but only / vaulting ambition, which o'er leaps itself …'. Clearly, strong ambition motivates him; such active words as 'vaulting' and 'o'er leap' suggest a move to action. However, he is fearful of failing to fulfil his ambition, as suggested by the repetition of the word 'fail' in the previous two quotations.

[C] Shakespeare's play *Macbeth* offers us an in-depth psychological study of the progress and effects of uncontrolled ambition. The central character, Macbeth, is not without aspirations and desires for power and greatness.

[D] As the play progresses, Macbeth's ambition is shown through the fact that he considers taking action in order to become king. This extract shows that he is considering his options in attaining the

When editing, check that the structure of your essay is logical.

dream of being king: 'The Prince of Cumberland! That is a step / On which I must fall down, or else o'er leap, / for in my way it lies'. He resolves that he must take action; that is, 'o'er leap' any obstacles.

[E] Shakespeare wrote Macbeth in the early 1600s and it is his third-shortest play. The play includes five acts. Throughout the play, Shakespeare develops some striking images around themes such as order versus disorder, illness versus health, and morality versus immorality.

[F] Macbeth's intention to become king progresses from leaving things to chance to deciding on taking personal action. By giving in to his outrageous ambition he becomes one of the most infamous murdering tyrants in literature.

1 The essay contains an irrelevant paragraph – identify it and explain its irrelevance.

2 The paragraphs in the essay are jumbled. Establish the correct order by organising the paragraph numbers.

3 Write the statement of the essay subject found in the introduction.

4 Write the topic sentence from Paragraph D.

5 **a** Write three synonyms in the essay used for the keyword *ambition*.

b Give two other synonyms for *ambition*.

6 Write a quotation used as evidence in the essay.

7 What type of introduction is used: historical/background context, paraphrase or quotation?

8 What type of conclusion is used: summary, caution or prediction?

Rewrite the first-draft essay below in the space provided, and do the following:

- → Separate the paragraphs. (There are four.)
- → Correct all the spelling errors. (There are eight.)
- → Add apostrophes of contraction. (There are three.)
- → Rewrite the run-on sentence as two separate sentences.
- → Correct all subject–verb agreement errors. (There are two.)
- → Identify one sentence (by crossing it out) that contains irrelevant information.

Doesnt the local council want teenagers to enjoy themselves? Recently, our local cownsel have been banning under-age club events. Last Saturday, the council cancelled an under-age disco 10 minutes before it was due to open. This left hundreds of teenagers stranded in the streets with nothing to do. Under-age events provide much-needed entertainment and releef from boredom for teenagers. Such events provide a fun and happy enviroment in which we can socialise and make new friends. As these events are closely supervised, teenagers can enjoy themselves in a safe, alcohol- and drug-free place. Closing down under-age venues doesnt make sense, when the council allows over-18 events with alchohol available to run until early morning when people leave in drunken states! Not only do under-age events raise money for the club and provide fundraising for teenage charity services, they add to the economic prosperity of surrounding buzinezes. Many teenagers buy their clubbing clothes at local shops others meet for dinner at local restoorants before attending the club. Maria's Pizza House offers a delicious menu in a smoke-free environment. These events also provide employment and training oppertunities for teenagers in the entertainment and hospitality industries. Teenagers has a chance to learn and to show what they can do as event organisers, DJs, models, dancers and singers. As a dancer at under-age events, I get to earn some pocket money as well as gain experience. Local teenagers feel let down by the poor attitoode of the council as there are many benefits to under-age events. If the council doesnt support underage events it could suffer a backlash in future elections when today's teenagers are voters!

SPELLING FOCUS

The following words appear in this unit. Add a tick next to the ones that are spelt correctly and a cross next to the ones that are spelt incorrectly. Write the correct spelling in the space next to the words spelt incorrectly.

enshore	[ ]		evidence	[ ]	
audience	[ ]		sircumstances	[ ]	
ambition	[ ]		entertainment	[ ]	
consistant	[ ]		canceled	[ ]	
alcohol	[ ]		busness	[ ]	
emphasise	[ ]		repitition	[ ]	
tirants	[ ]		imorality	[ ]	

Name: | Due date: | Guardian signature:

REVISION TEST 4

1 Read this Year 10 essay about a novel and complete the tasks that follow.

Essay question: Drawing on a text you have studied, discuss how loss affects people's lives.

James Moloney's rites of passage novel *Lost Property* explores the struggle for identity as well as the experience of personal loss. In this novel the idea of 'loss' means yearning for someone who has disappeared, or being lost in life. Loss can be deeply emotional or sentimental. It is widely accepted that loss can have various negative and positive effects on people's lives. There were several characters in the novel who demonstrate the different effects of loss, such as Josh, Michael, Carol and Clive. Josh is motivated by the idea of loss and lost things, which deeply affects his behaviour, thoughts and what he learns about life. Throughout the novel, Josh feels he has lost his identity and feelings of belonging in terms of family, friends, values and religion. Consequently, he is looking for 'lost' things in his life. He has philosophical thoughts about religion and the existence of God, which is encouraged by his conversations with Gemma. He wonders, "Is the universe the way it is because God made it that way, or simply because it happened that way?" This thought refers to the theme of questioning religious beliefs and faith, an experience of loss for Josh. He wonders whether the theory of God creating the universe is more believable than scientific principles. This reveals that Josh is deeply pensive but also cynical in dealing with his feelings of loss. Josh realises that he has lost faith in God and must break away from his father's values and opinions to gain his own identity. He chooses not to go to church with his family, which causes a change in his family relationships and a sense of loss for Josh. However, this sense of loss helps Josh grow up as he feels that he can stop acting and pretending to be someone he's not. In his case, this loss is difficult but it leads to his personal development. Further, Josh's actions are driven by his feelings of loss. He decides to travel to Mackay to find his runaway brother, Michael, and reconcile his broken family. This is conveyed by the quote, "I'd bring him back … what could have greater sentimental value to my family than Michael?" This shows that Josh feels that unity and happiness will be restored in his family if he brings his brother back. However, he learns that Michael's definition of happiness is different to his parents' and even his own. Josh learns that everyone finds their own version of happiness. This experience and lessons due to loss lead to Josh's maturation, which is clearly evident by the end of the novel. Michael's experience of loss is complicated as he has lost all direction and identity in his life. He felt that he had to leave home to regain these. He left his family because he felt he was pressured to act like his father and he couldn't live up to this expectation. He acted irresponsibly and rebelled against everything his parents expected of him because he wanted to prove his own individuality. This is confirmed when he said to Josh, "Sooner or later you have to make your own life. The best things in life are the ones you go out and grab for yourself … you'll have to break away from him [Phil, the father] in the end". This demonstrates that Michael wanted to step out of his father's shadow and gain his own identity and 'become his own man'. To do so, he felt that he needed to leave home and travel away from his past life to start one where he was away from his father's dominant influence. This created terrible loss for all of the family. However, in the end, loss affected Michael's life in a positive way as it helped him gain his own identity and learn more about life. The effect of loss in Carol's life is profound, as it has a destructive effect on her and strains her relationships with various family members because of her role as mother. Carol is devastated over Michael's disappearance. She felt like she had failed him as a mother, and blames herself for letting him go. This can be demonstrated through Phil's comment, "…[Carol] is always worried about that … that her mother's love wasn't strong enough, that the way things were such a mess for Michael was her fault". This implies that Carol has lost her sense of identity as a mother and is anguished. Loss also affects Carol's personal relationship with her husband, Phil. They have intense conflicts over Michael, which is demonstrated in the conversation where Carol says, "… you threw him out like a sack of garbage". This dialogue implies that Carol blames Phil for Michael's disappearance and feels betrayed by her husband. Phil's feeling of loss is dispassionate acceptance, a contrast to Carol's feelings and it adds to her sense of sadness. Loss clearly has a deep influence on Carol's life as she feels vulnerable, agonised and distraught by her experience. Subsequently, *Lost Property* shows that loss affects people's lives in a variety of ways. The characters in this novel who were most affected by loss were Josh, Michael and Carol. Josh's actions and thoughts were influenced by loss, whereas Michael found that he had to leave his family to restore the lost things in his life. The effect of loss was devastating and destructive on Carol's life. Therefore, it can be concluded that *Lost Property* successfully demonstrated that loss affects people's lives in a range of ways.

a Paraphrase the topic.

b The essay has six paragraphs. Identify each paragraph by adding a slash (/) at the start of the paragraph.

c Write a topic sentence from the essay.

d Write a concluding sentence from the essay.

e What type of introduction is used: paraphrase, historical context, anecdote or quotation?

f What type of conclusion is used: summary, caution, recommendation or prediction?

g Give an example from the essay of a quotation.

h Identify examples of vocabulary describing the personalities and feelings of characters used in the essay.

2 Write a sentence outlining your response to the essay topic.